BLACK
FLAG
OF THE
NORTH

VICTOR SUTHREN

BLACK FLAG
OF THE
NORTH

BARTHOLOMEW ROBERTS,
KING OF THE ATLANTIC PIRATES

DUNDURN
TORONTO

Cover image: Laura Boyle
Printer: Webcom

Library and Archives Canada Cataloguing in Publication

Suthren, Victor, 1942-, author
    Black flag of the north : Bartholomew Roberts, king of the Atlantic pirates / Victor Suthren.

Includes bibliographical references and index.
Issued in print and electronic formats.
ISBN 978-1-4597-3600-9 (softcover).--ISBN 978-1-4597-3601-6 (PDF).--
ISBN 978-1-4597-3602-3 (EPUB)

    1. Roberts, Bartholomew, 1682?-1722. 2. Pirates--Wales--Biography.
3. Biographies. I. Title.

G537.R74S88 2018   910.4'5   C2018-902153-5
                                             C2018-902154-3

1 2 3 4 5   22 21 20 19 18

We acknowledge the support of the **Canada Council for the Arts**, which last year invested $153 million to bring the arts to Canadians throughout the country, and the **Ontario Arts Council** for our publishing program. We also acknowledge the financial support of the **Government of Ontario**, through the **Ontario Book Publishing Tax Credit** and the **Ontario Media Development Corporation**, and the **Government of Canada**.

Nous remercions le **Conseil des arts du Canada** de son soutien. L'an dernier, le Conseil a investi 153 millions de dollars pour mettre de l'art dans la vie des Canadiennes et des Canadiens de tout le pays.

Care has been taken to trace the ownership of copyright material used in this book. The author and the publisher welcome any information enabling them to rectify any references or credits in subsequent editions.
                   — *J. Kirk Howard, President*

The publisher is not responsible for websites or their content unless they are owned by the publisher.

Printed and bound in Canada.

VISIT US AT

  dundurn.com | @dundurnpress | dundurnpress | dundurnpress

Dundurn
3 Church Street, Suite 500
Toronto, Ontario, Canada
M5E 1M2

For Scott, Caedi, and Amy,
and their beautiful families

Contents

I

Drawn to the Sea

In Pembrokeshire, in the wet and windy southwest corner of Wales, there stood in the last decades of the seventeenth century a small, impoverished village of a few houses with the unexpectedly grand name of Castell Newydd Bach, or Little Newcastle. Home to Welsh-speaking cattle herders of the green hills not far from the growing village of Haverfordwest, and, six miles farther south, the port of Milford Haven on its estuary leading to the Irish Sea, it was the unremarkable birthplace of a baby boy on May 17, 1682.

That small, squalling bundle occasioned little more in its anxious parents than gratitude that both mother and child had survived the rigours of the birth and gloomy awareness that, by the dreadful standards of mortality of the late seventeenth century, the child stood a fifty percent chance of not living past the age of three, and even less of reaching adulthood. The parents need not have worried: their lusty-lunged little son, christened John Robert or Roberts, would not only survive, but grow to strapping six-foot manhood and on faraway seas become the most feared and successful — if the word is appropriate — open-ocean pirate of the age. And it would be in what later became Canadian waters that he seized the tools that would have him appear out of the north in this role as uncrowned but de facto king of the Atlantic pirates.

In a brief, incandescent career from 1718 to 1722, he would take more than 450 ships and bring West Indian and African trade virtually to a standstill before dying in a hail of Royal Navy gunfire.

Yet there was little in the boy's background to suggest not an obscure life in the little houses and rain-soaked hills of Little Newcastle, but an eventual bloody career as a criminal terror of the seas. His father, identified as such in the Pembrokeshire Hearth Tax lists of 1670, was most probably known as George Robert — the change in spelling to *Roberts*, a common Welsh name, would come later.[1] His mother's name is unknown.

The little village was fervently religious in the manner of the rural Welsh, possibly adhering to the Calvinist rigour of the small Baptist community that had established itself in South Wales in the 1640s. That faith had to struggle to survive in the face of various Acts of Parliament intended to enforce the superiority of the Church of England. The villagers clung doggedly to their abstemious faith, the one small chapel "of the very meanest fashion" a centrepiece of the tiny community. And while English was increasingly the dominant language along the more populous coast to the south, the spare, devout lives of the Little Newcastle people were spent in a grimly surviving Welsh culture.

That is not to say that the Robert family were struggling paupers: there was at least home ownership, which made them akin to the English yeomen class. As historian Richard Sanders has expressed it, it was a status of "middle class, but in the context of a backward, rural society that was poor even by the standards of late seventeenth-century Britain."[2]

It was not an auspicious entry for the newest member of the Robert family, but the boy's later career as an otherwise-ruthless high-seas pirate would always be marked by a puritanical personal restraint and religiosity that had its roots in the dim, fervent world of rural faith in which he was raised.

The nature of life for the poor Welsh was only marginally different from what it had been in the Middle Ages: subsistence farming and animal husbandry tied to the ebb and flow of the seasons, and now marked by a reticence and suspicion of the non-Welsh who increasingly were settling the Pembrokeshire coast. Historian R.J. Hammond observes:

There was one small part of the Principality whose history branches off in Norman times — that part of southern Pembrokeshire known as "Little England Beyond Wales." This is where the followers of William the Conqueror had some success and they settled their tiny gains with Flemings, refugees from the flooding of the Low Countries. They were reinforced in the time of Henry the Second who brought Flemish soldiers to settle in Wales and interspersed them with Englishmen in order that they should learn to speak English.[3]

There is an image of the South Welsh that persists from that age: a short, stocky people of swarthy, almost Mediterranean appearance — the "Silures" of the Romans — keeping to their valleys and uplands in ever more heightened suspicion of the English after the great Civil War, when the Welsh had remained largely Royalist, sustained by their nonetheless Nonconformist faith and the unfathomable intricacies of their ancient language: a musical, poetic, darkly serious people with a deep historical sense of loss, an enduring resilience in the face of hardship and want, and their suspicions of the tan-haired strangers on the coast. It was a close, emotional tribal culture akin to that of Scots Highland clans or the wild countrymen of Ireland, and to a lad of modest means it was also characterized by an outdoor life of physical harshness that would go a long way to prepare him for the rigours of the sea. George Owen, a member of modest Welsh gentry at the time, is quoted by Richard Sanders:

> I have by good account numbered 3,000 young people to be brought up continually in herding of cattle within this shire who are put to this idle education when they are first come to be ten or twelve years of age … They are forced to endure the heat of the sun in his greatest extremity, to parch and burn their faces, hands, legs, feet and breasts, in such sort as they seem more like tawny Moors than people of this land, and then the cold, frost, snow, hail, rain and wind. They are so tormented, having

the skin of their legs, hands, face and feet all in chinks and chaps.[4]

The influence of religion in the shaping of young Roberts — for such we may begin to call him — is markedly similar to the preparation of another extraordinary seafarer who would emerge decades later, and go on to greater notice, albeit of a markedly different and admired kind: Pacific navigator James Cook. Cook spent much of his formative youth in the company of Yorkshire Quakers, and it was noted of him during his later remarkable voyages of discovery that he was never known to have succumbed to the allure of rum — unlike almost anyone who sailed with him — nor did he share in the sexual contact with Pacific island women when his crews did, virtually to a man. Roberts would be marked by the same restraint, even as he led crews of hardened men characterized by almost no restraint at all. For Roberts, as for Cook, there would be no drunken revels or sexual profligacy, and if both men came to this remarkable restraint due to the strong role religion played in their lives, it would give them incalculable strength through social distance in their leadership of their rough-hewn men. That one bound himself by a sense of duty to the legalities of society and the other set himself at war with those legalities does not mask that they approached the tricky business of leading men in harsh pursuits from the same place. One would die respected and honoured, destined for an admiral's flag and a knighthood, had he lived; the other died reviled as a criminal, and destined to the shame of the gibbet, had he lived to be captured. But both men had the qualities of which leadership is made, in remarkably similar ways.

For the Welsh, the slow progress into a resolute Protestantism was aided by the 1588 translation of the Bible into Welsh, and the efforts of the Welsh Tudor Elizabeth I to ensure Catholicism would not dominate Britain. That struggle would not be resolved until the "Great Revolution" of 1688, but, during the 1640s and 1650s, and the struggles of the bitter Civil War, the Welsh were paradoxically dogged supporters of the Crown. By 1647, though, the parliamentary army had crushed dissent in both North and South Wales. The exception would be the town of Pembroke, near Milford Haven, which remained a lonely outpost of parliamentary support — and with likely an English rather than a Welsh mentality. Why the Welsh embraced Nonconformist religion, much like the men of Parliament, yet remained suspicious of their motives, and, like the Loyalists of the American Revolution, "would rather be governed by one tyrant three thousand miles away than three thousand tyrants one mile away," may have its roots in the same Celtic survival mentality that characterized both the Irish and the Highland Scots. Whatever its effect, it gave young John Roberts a unique, almost tribal sense of differing identity in the British world, and seems to have anchored it with an abstemious religiosity in his personal ways even as he led amoral and bloodthirsty "lost" men in a fiery career of theft, destruction, and violence: a life of being, in a very real sense, an outsider at war with all the world.

How a cattle-herding boy of the Welsh hinterland could become the seaman and leader he did is subject to much speculation, as almost no records exist of the period between his birth in 1682 and his reappearance at sea in his midthirties as a capable open-ocean mariner. With Milford Haven within walking distance of his village and the increasing pace of shipping offering much to entice a likely lad beyond the mucking-out of byres, it may be that, again like James Cook, who fled his barnyard boyhood to follow the sea, Roberts — we can begin calling him Bartholomew, as he seems to have been known at sea — came to the coast to seek his fortune afloat.

Already a strapping six-footer, in contrast to the short stature so common in South Wales then, he would have stood out as a prime candidate for an apprenticeship as a seaman in one of the many coastal vessels sailing from Milford Haven. Roberts appears years later, in 1718, as a capable Second or Third Mate of a 140-ton slaver — one account claims him to be a carpenter, a valuable man on any wooden ship — and the question arises whether he had grown to manhood with his evident skills solely in the grim world of the slave ship.[5]

That seems unlikely. As historian Marcus Rediker points out,

> Slave-trade seamen came from numerous social backgrounds, from orphanages and jails to respectable working-class and even middle-class families. But sailors

as a whole were widely known as among the poorest occupational groups in Britain and America in the eighteenth century, so there were many more of the former group than the latter. Indeed [a writer] described slave-trade seamen as "the refuse and dregs of the Nation," refugees of the "prisons and glass houses." He added that most "have generally been bred to it young" … but some were also "boys impatient of their parents or masters" … and men "already ruin'd by some untimely vice" … The "white slaves" who served aboard [slave] ships were essentially the "very dregs of the community."[6]

In sharp contrast, the Roberts of 1718 was somehow literate, having evidently mastered navigation (as his later career would show), and had a number of other skills, fighting and otherwise, which it is hard to imagine were won in long residence in the fetid mess decks of a Guineaman, as slavers were known. The life of a seaman of the day commonly involved a period of service — voluntary or not — in one of His Britannic Majesty's warships, which, during the War of the Spanish Succession (1701–14) were hungry for men "trained for the sea," and anyone wishing to be. The apparent truth of the matter is that by 1718, when Roberts appears for the first time in any kind of formal historical record, he was a competent and skilled open-ocean mariner of strength and a commanding presence who knew how to lead men and how to "fight" a ship: to use its guns and sailing tactics to defeat an enemy at sea. Such skills were learned in privateers, of course, but more readily in disciplined warships, and when, after 1713, Roberts may have conceivably been among the many paid-off navy crews looking for work afloat, he was a prime candidate: many others, less fortunate, would be left ashore to poverty and beggary. It can reasonably be argued that it was in navy service that he learned the critical skills, like many other pirates in the turbulent postwar world — including the fearsome and legendary "Blackbeard," Edward Teach. Why Roberts would opt for the dark world of the slave ships instead of a merchant vessel is not clear: his circumstances at the time are not known. He may have been glad of any opportunity.

The Royal Navy that conceivably either swept up young Roberts in its "press" or received his volunteer service had gone through a varied period of strength and decline, from its heady days of success under Cromwell to the humiliation of the Dutch raids of the 1660s, and an uncertain degree of national support through the last years of the seventeenth century. By Queen Anne's time and the beginning of the War of the Spanish Succession, the navy had benefitted from some reforms brought about by James II and a shipbuilding program initiated by King William in 1690. By the time war broke out in 1702, the Royal Navy was at least as strong as the French navy, and was concentrating on acting in concert with the now allied Dutch. It would produce some significant victories, notably the capture of Port Mahon on Minorca and the natural fortress of Gibraltar. Although many thousands of men served in the navy until peace in 1713, it was not a war of many massive fleet actions, but more one of manoeuvring, seamanship, gunnery, and smaller ship-to-ship encounters. The war ended with Britain in commercial and naval control of the Atlantic and the Mediterranean, but with the war's end many warships were "paid off" and their highly trained crews — Roberts arguably among them — were released into the uncertain peacetime world in their thousands, competing for berths in merchant shipping, the fishing fleets, or, as a last resort, the slave ships. To their numbers would have been added the men who crewed in privateer vessels; civilian warships under licence from the Crown to prey on enemy shipping for profit. The major sea powers' preoccupation with the war had left few resources for suppressing the endemic piracy that bedevilled western European sea commerce. Ironically, the peacetime freedom to turn naval attention to the scourge of piracy came just as thousands of capable recruits for that criminal life, who could find no legitimate employment at sea, were released into the lawless open-ocean environment — where piracy was arguably their final option.

If Roberts was indeed shaped into a fighting leader by service in the navy, the nature of that institution at the time is worth examining. The navy of Queen Anne would become, through the War of the Spanish Succession, Britain's principal instrument of policy and "national extension" into the coldly competitive international world. In the time of Elizabeth I, the ships maintained by the Crown had formed only a fraction of those available, or necessary, for the defence of the British Isles, or the extension of the Crown's policies against England's principal adversaries. The English fleet that harried the Spanish Armada through its disastrous 1588 attempt at invasion was primarily a private one, over which the Crown had imprecise and unpredictable control. Through the seventeenth century, through Cromwell's Commonwealth, and then under the Stuarts, the transition was made from a small core of Royal vessels around which a temporary fleet could assemble to a permanently established Royal Navy funded by Parliament that acted in accordance with the wishes and intent of the Crown and government. Other European nations established national navies, some before Britain, but geographic necessity ensured that Britain's navy was, in the main, the most successful. That success was by no means certain in the seventeenth century, and would build only toward the end of the eighteenth.

In 1702, when Roberts would have been entering his twenties, Britain maintained a fleet of several hundred proper warships, or "men of war." These were supported by a wide range of auxiliary vessels and an established dockyard system that was intended to maintain both operational vessels and those that were laid up in reserve, or "in ordinary." These warships were very roughly divided between those ships considered large enough to take a meaningful role in a major battle formation — to "lie in the line" and thus be a "ship of the line" — and those considered too small to do so. In the era of Queen Anne, the principal armament of British warships were batteries of cast iron, or occasionally bronze, smoothbore muzzle-loading guns carried on one or more decks of the ship and set in rows to fire out through "gun ports" along the ship's side. These were fired by black powder charges loaded into the guns along with the cast-iron round "shot" they propelled, by a team of up to a dozen seamen commanded by a gun captain. The shot was of graduating sizes measured in pounds of their weight, and the gun was known by the weight of the ball it fired: a "24-pounder" was a gun that fired a ball weighing twenty-four pounds, and so on.

A variety of projectiles were used, including balls linked by chain to cut through rigging; bags of smaller balls called "grape" to fire at human targets; and bar shot, halves of round shot linked by a bar and meant to cartwheel through the air and strike crew and ship alike.

In a "broadside" — the firing together of all the guns on one side of a warship — the larger vessels could hurl up to a half-ton of metal to an extreme distance of three miles, with a rate of fire often as fast as two rounds in three minutes. The principal aim of ship combat, which pirates sought to avoid at all costs, as they wished to remain healthy in a functioning ship, was to batter the enemy into submission by inflicting either casualties to the crew or damage to the ship (or, rarely, by sinking it). The line-of-battle formation was the standard means of presenting all vessels' broadsides for maximum effect against a similar enemy formation. Smaller vessels, usually those with fewer than sixty guns, were often sent on lone patrols as scouts for the larger formation, and the handiest and most active of these were the nimbler vessels known as "frigates," which might carry as few as twenty guns. The family of warships was organized into six "rates," with the giant, hundred-gun battleships being "first-rate" warships and the lowly eighteen-gun sloop being a "sixth-rate."

By the time Roberts went to sea, the ships were remarkable summations of almost three hundred years of European ocean-going experience, if the Viking period is discounted. Acres of oak forest were felled to provide the timber for the hulls. Miles of rope-work and cordage, acres of canvas, and a complex pantheon of craftsmen's skills went into producing each ship, whether a merchantman or a warship. The most fleet and beautiful designs were traditionally French and Spanish, while the sturdiest of construction, if dull in performance, were English or Dutch. Vessels like the coastal traders, which conceivably were Roberts's first experience at sea, could be sailed by five or six able men, controlling sails and rigging with a complex series of pulleys and tackles, while a vast battleship could be crammed with seven hundred men to ensure she could be sailed and "fought" at the same time. The vessels were taken to sea and operated there by "sea officers," which is to say professional seamen, by the end of the seventeenth century and the reign of Queen Anne. They were controlled by the Admiralty and supplied by a separate and often maddeningly independent Navy Board.

The organizational leadership, sense of discipline, and orderly conduct that Roberts would display in his piratical career, even leading men to whom such things were anathema, and which lay at the heart of his successful career, are telling signs, in the view of this writer, of his exposure at some point in his life to the ordered world of a seagoing warship's society. The key elements of that society were the body of competent sea officers below the captain, who aspired to their own commands one day, and the prime seamen, from Able Seaman to Sailing Master, who did the physical work that made the ship operate. The former were meant to command and navigate; the latter to obey, and to sail the vessel under direction. The distinction between officer and man was, by 1700, becoming great, socially: the former entered the navy, and left it, voluntarily; the latter, if he did not volunteer, could be pressed into service and he was released only if the navy saw fit to do so. Press gangs scoured shore ports for victims to feed into the navy's endlessly man-hungry system in wartime, and once in the navy the newcomer entered a brutal and regulated world that offered little sympathy for the disinclined. It was a cruel and callous age to later eyes, with capital punishment in society ashore a common penalty for the most trifling of crimes. In the Royal Navy, discipline and deference to authority were enforced with the lash. Admiral Edward Vernon, writing a generation later, would say that the navy was manned by violence and maintained by cruelty. Yet, as an institution, it was able to inspire the mostly young men who formed it to fight with fierce spirit, or endure astonishing hardships. It was a hard, utterly unforgiving society, mirroring perhaps both the fatalism of the age and the indifferent menace of the sea. In addition to the risk of death by drowning or enemy action, the seaman faced the greatest killer, disease, accompanied by ignorance, crowded mess decks, monotonous food, and an appalling lack of sanitation in modern terms, which would only begin to be addressed in the navy a half-century later.

The sailor owned few possessions, though an officer might fill a small cabin with his. He kept them in a seabag or seachest, to which he had limited access. He slept in a hammock, an invention borrowed from Caribbean native society two hundred years earlier, slung at night beneath the beams over the long row of guns, and put away into netting on deck during the day. He wore no uniform — one would not be ordered for the Royal Navy until 1748, and then only for officers — and, dependent upon the character of the ship's captain and his supply officer, or "purser," he could be clothed in the rags he joined with or be clad in sturdy, standard clothing bought from the ship and known as "slops." A kind of standard dress had developed, largely from practicality. It featured long trousers or kilt-like "petticoat breeches," as well as the standard knee breeches of the era, and shorter jackets rather than the long, full-skirted coats that had come into style at the end of the century. A colour scheme of red and grey for the "slops" clothing was gradually moving into the colours blue and white. At sea the sailor wore snug woollen or fur caps, tarred or oiled jackets and watch coats, thick woollen pullovers, and an ever-present sheath knife on a lanyard or belt, its tip frequently blunted (if the captain so decreed) to keep him from knifing his messmate. He went barefoot in all but the most inclement weather, to save precious and expensive shoes and to give him sure footing aloft or on wet, pitching decks. His hands and feet soon became hard, horn-surfaced black claws, stained with tar and scarred from endless cuts and hurts from sails and rigging. Ashore, his swaying walk and seaman's clothes gave him away, as did his darkly tanned face, sometimes marked with gunpowder tattoos of hearts and anchors, and his hair, worn long and unbound as was the custom, but increasingly clubbed back into a long, Chinese-style queue. He carried a sturdy stick to cudgel any landsman that "crossed his bows," and his pockets jingled, albeit briefly, with the coin that delighted both tavern keeper and prostitute alike.

Powerfully muscular in his prime due to the sheer strength required in work at sea, the seaman was frequently ruptured (lower-body hernias caused by extreme strain), but no evidence exists that this afflicted Roberts. If the sailor lived through the rigours of his calling, he was normally exhausted and worn out by forty-five, destined for a beggar's life ashore unless he had managed to save some of his meagre pay. (Regular pay had been established under Charles II.) By nature he was open and trusting with his shipmates, notoriously cheerful and superstitious, and an easy mark for both the cruelty of brutal captains and the social predators of the portside towns. He followed good officers with stunning loyalty and endurance, proud of his tenacity and ability to withstand difficulty; he endured bad officers, whether naval or merchant, with long tolerance, striking back rarely and only when deeply provoked; and he considered himself worth three soldiers or ten French or Spanish.

Though many men survived careers at sea and left with a small nest egg gathered with prudence to buy a small farm or even an inn, more commonly the sailor spent his pay or rare "prize money" — his share of the value of captured vessels after they were sold — as soon as it was in his hands, funding the legions of prostitutes and rows of alehouses that were his refuge when he was trusted to go ashore, and where he awaited the next press gang. Stereotypically ignorant, childish, honourable, generous, brutal, and brotherly by turns, with his unmistakable rolling gait and his mahogany skin, the Royal Navy or merchant seaman into whose society Roberts may have entered at the beginning of the 1702–13 war was a unique creature in many ways; almost another species from the landsmen of the British Isles. And when he gave up on the world's lawful ways of doing things, he was a formidable enemy indeed.

The captain set above such men in a naval vessel had reached that position through a long apprenticeship that had seen him join a vessel as a youth and serve as a midshipman, and possibly even a servant or common seaman before that. After this he would take his Board to be passed for a lieutenant, and in that rank to serve as one of the several officers of the ship, waiting until death, disease, war, or good fortune allowed him to become the captain of a major vessel. The term used was *Post Captain*, and to be "made post" was to enter not only into the command of a vessel of note, but also that fraternity whose members might, with luck, end their careers, or their lives, as admirals. The accident of birth, nobility, or privilege did not guarantee seamanship, and as often impeded it. The navy needed sea officers for its ships, and few who could manage by societal standing or income to obtain a life of greater ease would enter the hard school of a naval vessel, or a harshly run merchantman, where little other than competence could bring about career success. The navy, and the merchant service to a degree, was one place in a tightly structured and unfair society where personal merit and the ability to learn an art — and withstand its rigours — would allow a man to aspire to goals commensurate with his skills.

In the world of the common seaman, a man would find himself organized for the ship's duties into a "watch." One portion, or "watch," of the ship's crew operated the vessel while another portion was off duty. Typically, a watch was on duty for four hours, with then four or eight hours off. Two two-hour watches around dusk, known, oddly, as "dogwatches," ensured a rotation that kept watches from being on duty at the same time each day. While on watch a seaman could be set to any number of tasks, usually involved in maintaining the ship or operating it. For special tasks, and for crisis situations such as action against another ship, the seaman was assigned a place on the "Watch and Quarter Bill." These lists, usually penned laboriously by the captain's clerk and pinned up on the lower decks or the "fo'c'sle" (the forecastle, where the men lived), might detail a man to be part of the crew of a particular gun, when in action; to row a certain oar in the longboat, if it was called away; to be armed with a cutlass, and board another ship from forward in close action, and so on. Overriding these were, for warships, orders from the Crown and the Admiralty, the Articles of War, and the orders of the captain and the ship's officers. Life was a highly regulated process, and penalties for failure were severe, brutal, and often fatal unless mitigated by compassion and humanity, which were all too rare.

The seaman was also made part of a family of sorts in being assigned to a "mess," a unit of perhaps ten men who, in warships, lived in the space between two guns on a long-gun deck, where they slung their hammocks from overhead beams off-watch, kept communal possessions and a few personal things, and ate together around rope-slung tables when the "cook," a man detailed to bring the food to his mess from the "galley," ladled out the often distasteful but usually adequate food. A man's mess was both home and family, and in the order of loyalty a messmate ranked famously before a shipmate, a shipmate before a landsman, a landsman before a dog, and a dog before a soldier(!). It would be another half-century before regiments of seagoing soldiery called "marines" would be constituted as part of the navy, to soon earn the sailor's respect. With his messmates, the sailor was utterly without privacy, even when attending to natural functions, and the great unspoken struggle for each man was to find a few moments of personal space: aloft in the rigging, in the lee of the longboat, anywhere. The close society of a ship sandpapered away the layered pretences of the landsman; joined to the pitiless rigour of the seaman's work, it soon brought home to a man, and those who knew him, the realities of his strengths, his weaknesses, and his character to a degree not always understood by those ashore. More readily understandable was the appalling nature of the food the seaman was obliged to eat, ranging from weevil-ridden and rocklike "bread" — in reality a kind of granitic biscuit — to equally tough salted beef and pork kept in casks, and precious few vegetables. The horrifying disease of scurvy, which we now know is caused by vitamin C deficiency, was little understood then and the scourge of the seaman. Water was usually so foul in the casks that men were issued a gallon of "small" (that is, weak) beer a day, and a daily portion of brandy or, more usually, dark West Indian rum, served out undiluted and not as the watered version called "grog" issued a half-century later. Though poor by modern standards, the nutrition available to the common seaman of Roberts's era was likely no worse than that available to people of an equal class ashore, and a degree of toughness and endurance unimaginable today contributed not a little to a seaman's survival in the face of such daunting daily odds.

Besides the gentlemen officers in the organization of a ship, there were the specialists: common seamen or artisans who had risen to a more senior status through experience and mastery of a technical art. Among these were the carpenter — Roberts was said to have been skilled as one — the gunner; the sailmaker; the boatswain, who looked after the ship's gear; and the Sailing Master, a kind of senior petty officer who was the authority for technically handling the ship in response to the navigational or tactical needs of the captain and his handful of lieutenants. These men, in the navy, held "warrants," as opposed to commissions, which acknowledged their technical ability and gave them status over the seamen, but denied them the status of gentlemen. They berthed forward or below with the men, in thin, canvas-walled temporary cabins set up amidst the guns and hammocks, while the gentlemen berthed aft, took their meals at servants' hands in the wardroom — except for the captain, who ate alone — and were joined by others allowed gentlemanly status such as the surgeon and chaplain.[7]

It was in the way that Roberts — when he became Bartholomew Roberts, and commanded his own ships — conducted himself and the operation of his ships, despite the seeming lawlessness and egalitarianism of pirate society, that we arguably see the effect of experience in a naval vessel. Roberts, as will be seen, famously introduced a code of conduct called the "Articles" that have a whiff of ship's regulations and even the Articles of War about them. In his leadership style, even though serving at the crew's pleasure, Roberts established a social distance between himself and his men, through distinctive, almost gentlemanly dress and abstention from drink and debauchery, all of which bespeak to this writer a familiarity with the social and behavioural norms that allowed Queen Anne's warships to function.

If, however, Bartholomew Roberts did not learn his seaman's calling as one of the "people" in a Royal Navy vessel, the other opportunities open to a farm youth drawn to the sea would have been varying forms of apprenticeship in one of the proliferating coastal vessels that connected communities with one another and the outside world, contemporary roads being at best muddy tracks requiring days of tedious and dangerous travel. Entering the world of the seaman in a merchant vessel exposed the newcomer to an existence less structured, but more exhausting and subject to greater misuses of authority than that aboard a Queen's ship, where there was at least the veneer of regulations to fall back on. As will be seen, mistreatment of seamen by merchant captains subject to no rigid regulating authority was a prime reason otherwise reliable seamen escaped into the dead end of piracy in desperation. Admittedly, there was not the oppressive weight of the Articles of War that meant death or appalling punishment for a range of "crimes," and less likelihood of being forced to remain in a ship for years at a time to prevent desertion. These alone guaranteed that men "using the sea" did everything possible to avoid being pressed into service in a naval vessel, unless they were making a deliberate choice of the navy. But in so many other aspects of life at sea, the merchant seaman was in a school of adversity that ensured either a speedy demise or a hardened proficiency in the sailor's arts, married to a brutality-edged survival instinct. The merchant mariner, like the naval "tar," inhabited a demanding world not lenient to the unenthusiastic. It bred hard, resilient men, of which Bartholomew Roberts clearly was an example, and he may have come to that state, and subsequently to piracy, at least partly because of a fatalism bred in a trade that was characterized by harshness unimaginable in the modern era.

Historian Marcus Rediker, writing in 2004, observed that working conditions in merchant and naval ships increasingly have been seen as the root cause of piracy in the years following the close of war in 1713 by the Treaty of Utrecht. He quotes at length the unnamed author of a contemporary pamphlet on the causes of piracy, who in turn quoted an "Officer of an East India Company Ship" who asserted that in addition to "general depravation of Seamens manners, and their little or no sense of religion," there were far more trenchant reasons why seamen fled the merchant or naval service for a life of crime.

> [B]ut he also relayed the reasons pirates had given, all of which turned on the brutalities of work at sea: impressment, beatings, poor food, and the disabling and deadly effects of these on themselves and their families. Some pirates cited "being drubb'd and beaten unmercifully by their Officers." "Such as had Sail'd in Merchants Ships," the officer continued, "complain'd of the barbarity of their Commanders, especially in depriving them of their sustenance."[8]

Rediker sums up efficiently the realities confronting the common seaman of the first years of the eighteenth century, when Bartholomew Roberts was presumably mastering his trade.

> Seafaring was one of the most dangerous occupations of a dangerous occupational age, with causes both natural and man-made. A common saying among sailors was, "There was the pox above-board, the plague between decks, hell in the forecastle, and the devil at the helm" … [I]n this period dangers of the sailors' workplace produced an endless array of mutilated bodies, evident in

every port city as sailors lame and crippled begged hither and yon.[9]

The question of why Roberts should have been drawn to such an existence remains unanswered, except that it may have been no more brutal to him than a hardscrabble life ashore, and did offer the prospect of some kind of adventure, or even the chance of fortune. Roberts clearly survived and even thrived in this harsh world, and that he did so says much about his personal qualities of endurance, toughness, and indifference to discomfort. In describing another pirate, Rediker provides what could easily be, at least in part, a portrait of Roberts as he heaves into view out of the haze of history in 1718, third mate of a slave ship on the West African coast, and about to embark on a momentous change in his hard-edged life:

> He was born into poverty in a port city; he was experienced in the rough conditions of life at sea, in both the navy and the merchant service; he was apparently unmarried; and he was in his mid-twenties. These traits served as bases of unity with others when, in search of something better, he decided to become a pirate. And yet he, like the others, was not merely escaping oppressive circumstances. He was escaping to something new, a different reality, something alluring about which he had heard tales in his youth.[10]

Something similar had undoubtedly drawn Bartholomew Roberts from the rainy obscurity of Welsh farm life to an almost unimaginably different life, but as he steps into view, it is as a practitioner of a foul and cruel industry, if a legal one, and as one about to depart that life for one of outright criminality and more immediate violence. The quiet green hills and the sombre little chapel of Little Newcastle were now far, far away. We have a brief description of Roberts's emergence into history from his biographer, Stanley Richards:

In 1718 he was mate of a Barbados sloop in the day when the grotesque Blackbeard was riding roughshod along the coast of the Americas, bringing havoc to shipping and plantations. In the Spring of 1719 [Roberts] sailed from London to the Guinea Coast … of West Africa, as third mate of the *Princess* galley, with Captain Abraham Plumb of Stepney parish as Master. The *Princess* had been licenced by the Royal African Company of London to transport slaves from the coast to the Americas.[11]

Whatever had drawn Roberts to the sea, he appears on it now in recorded history, a fully formed seaman of thirty-seven years, skilled and with authority, and engaged in a dark enterprise that would unexpectedly lead him to another endeavour, and his brief but colourful fate. That dark enterprise now is in view.

2

A Dark Enterprise

When Bartholomew Roberts arrived on the coast of West Africa in the *Princess* galley, he was preparing to participate — if he had not already done so a great deal — in the slave trade, which involved the transportation of African slaves to Spanish and Portuguese colonies, and later British and French territories, in the Americas. The trade was to provide workers to replace the decimated or unwilling native tribes pressed into service in the Europeans' mines and plantations. Europe had seen slavery in its societies as early as the Middle Ages, although on a small scale, and the memory of the Romans' slave systems was not lost. Nonetheless, by the time of the European expansion of the slave trade short decades after the rediscovery of the Americas, the trade had become a cornerstone of the rapidly evolving mercantilist economies of western European nations. Historian Herbert Klein has observed:

> The Atlantic slave trade was one of the most complex economic enterprises known to the preindustrial world. It was the largest transoceanic migration in history up to that time; it promoted the transportation of people and goods among three different continents; [and] involved an annual fleet of several hundred ships.[1]

It would be, however, a misconception to view the slave trade across the Atlantic as the genesis of the phenomenon of slavery on the African continent. It had been in existence well before the questing caravels of the Portuguese first coasted southward along the African coast in the late 1400s. Klein summarizes:

> Although large-scale commercial use of slaves was limited, the use of slaves within most African societies was widespread. The existence of this large number of slaves meant that a lively internal slave market and intracontinental slave trade existed. Thus, a dual slave trade came into existence well before the opening of the West African–Atlantic routes. Through the north and to the east, slaves were being shipped outside Africa in steady numbers for at least some six centuries prior to the arrival of the Portuguese.... For both these long-term trades, the whole complex of enslavement practices from full-scale warfare and raiding of enemies to judicial enslavement and taxation of dependent peoples had come into use and would easily be adjusted to the needs of the Atlantic slave trade when this came into existence in the early fifteenth century.[2]

Even given the existence of slavery before any significant European arrival on the coast of West Africa, the question arises as to how Europeans managed to impose their wills upon not only the conquered peoples of the Americas, but also on the coastal societies of the West African source of slaves. European goods soon convinced slaveholding African societies that a mutually profitable trade could develop. That the Europeans could create a market for slaves; command a source of them (to a degree); and then create a transportation and logistics system to connect the two was based on specific technological developments in western European societies, part of a general outburst of scientific and technical advance that had arisen not only from the innovative spirit of the Renaissance but also from the appetite for Eastern goods that had been made scarce by the Ottomans' capture of Constantinople in 1453 and the closure of the Levant to most Western trade. The Europeans were pushed to develop ship technology, navigation, and weaponry to regain access to the luxuries of the Middle East. But all that soon led to far more, as Marcus Rediker explains (paraphrasing Carlo Cipolla):

> Western European states were able to conquer the world between 1400 and 1700 because of two distinct and soon powerfully combined technological developments ... forged cast-iron cannon ... [and] the deep-sea sailing "round ship" of Northern Europe.... [W]hen the full-rigged ship equipped with muzzle-loading cannon showed up on the coasts of Africa, Asia, and America, it was by all accounts a marvel if not a terror....
>
> European rulers would use this revolutionary technology, this new maritime machine, to sail, explore, and master the high seas in order to trade, to fight, to seize new lands, to plunder, and to build empires.[3]

By the early eighteenth century the major European nations were wedded to the mercantilist concept of national economy, which viewed conquered territories or colonies, and their produce, raw materials, and mined wealth, as a necessary flow of value to the home country, and those territories as recipients or purchasers of the goods produced by that home country. Thriving sugar, tobacco, rice, and banana industries, to name but a few, in the newly established colonies were thus a vital source of national wealth, and needed an inexhaustible supply of cheap labour to produce it. This was a principal reality of the roughly two and a half centuries, 1600 to 1850, that were the high point of the transatlantic slave trade, in which ships would sail from a European — and later North or South American — port with cargos of manufactured goods to West Africa, where they were traded for slaves; then, via the middle passage crossing to the Americas, where they sold the slaves, and traded for products of the plantations, such as rum, molasses, sugar, tobacco, and rice; and a final voyage with those goods to the home markets. It was, as Rediker and others have pointed out, the notion of a triangular trade, which "remains valuable, because it permits a visualization of the three essential corners and components of the trade — [European] capital and manufactures, West African labor power, and American commodities (sometimes raw materials)."[4]

The tidiness of this concept and its profitability in the minds of the laced and bewigged investors in the European counting houses came at a cost, however. That cost was the exploitation of human life in a system of cruelty and dislocation that lay at the heart of their profits, to a degree astonishing to students already aware of the callous brutality that characterized seventeenth and early eighteenth century European society and endeavour. Rediker paints a grim picture:

> Scholars now estimate that, depending on time and place, some portion between a tenth and a half of the captives perished between the point of enslavement and the boarding of the slave ship.... From stage to stage — expropriation in Africa, the Middle Passage, initial exploitation in America — roughly 5 million men, women, and children died. Another way to look at the loss of life would be to say that an estimated 14 million people were enslaved to produce a "yield" of 9 million longer-surviving enslaved Atlantic workers.[5]

Beginning with the end of the Stuart era and continuing to the end of the eighteenth century, principally British shipping merchants based in Liverpool, Bristol, and other ports sent slaving vessels to collect their cargo in six basic regions of Africa: Sierre Leone, or the Windward Coast; Senegambia; the Gold Coast; the Bight of Benin; the Bight of Biafra; and West Central Africa. The term *Guinea* was used generally for all of these. Although Brazil had figured hugely as the principal market for slaves after the trade's inception, by the early to mid-eighteenth century it was the British sugar cane islands that had become the key buyers. There was also a continuing trade with the Spanish colonies through a special treaty arrangement called the *Asiento*, which allowed North European slave ships to supply slaves to buyers in Central and South America.[6]

When Bartholomew Roberts's *Princess* galley arrived off West Africa, it was part of a rapidly growing fleet, which, by 1720, had nearly 150 ships involved, most from Bristol and London.[7]

The *Asiento* was no small business. In the first twenty-five years of the eighteenth century, British slavers delivered over seventy-five thousand surviving slaves into Spanish American ports.[8] It had been growing British naval and economic power that had allowed such an arrangement to be imposed upon the unwilling Spanish. Slave trade historian Hugh Thomas summarizes the arrangement's importance:

> In 1707, the British government, largely to satisfy the [Royal Africa Company], drew up a draft contract between Queen Anne and the Archduke Charles, the British candidate to be king of Spain, to supply slaves to the Spanish Empire....
>
> The British maintained their pressure on Spain. By 1710, they were selling well over ten thousand slaves a year to the Indies, the Spanish Empire included....
>
> [W]hen the Treaty of Utrecht came to be drawn up in 1713, to conclude the War of the Spanish Succession, the British were able to insist on taking over the *asiento*. Though a Bourbon ruled in Madrid, British ships would carry Africans to the Americas to work in the haciendas, the palaces, the mines, and the tobacco and sugar farms of his great empire.[9]

At first through the commercial body known as the Royal Africa Company — which had contracted Roberts's *Princess* — and later with an additional company known as the South Sea Company, which in turn contracted to transport the slaves acquired by the Royal Africa Company, the British established fortified posts on the African coasts, as did other European slavers. Here they soon began to amass the wretched victims of the thriving domestic African slave culture, and in so doing set up profitable relations with middleman West African societies. These were only too happy to provide cargos for the waiting ships in return for European goods or money. As Rediker and other slave trade historians point out, it was soon an ambitious commercial enterprise for all concerned:

> The English operated forts and trading establishments at Dixcove, Sekondi, Komenda, Anomabu, Accra, and Tantum; the seat of their operations was Cape Coast Castle. From these outposts traders loaded prisoners — black gold — into the lower decks of the ships. The building of the forts gave rise to ministates....
>
> The mightiest group in the region was the Asante, whose rise after 1680 resulted in one of the strongest stratified and centralized states of West Africa.[10]

In addition to the demands of the *Asiento*, the growing demand for more slaves in the profitable Caribbean sugar islands led the South Sea Company to begin establishing "receiving ports" for the arrival of the slave ships and that part of their wretched cargos that had survived the voyage. Thomas observes:

> The South Sea Company agreed to buy in Africa the slaves required from the old RAC; take them to Jamaica ... and then carry the prime slaves to Spanish markets.... [A] third of the company's ships would go to Loango Bay, a quarter to the Gold Coast, a little less to Dahomey, and the rest mostly set off for Senegambia....
>
> The new South Sea Company established factories at Barbados ... and at Port Royal, Jamaica.[11]

In short, the transatlantic slave trade was an extensive, well-funded commercial operation supporting investors in Britain and elsewhere in Europe, the plantation owners in the Americas and the Caribbean, and the shipping owners who sent their vessels on the round of the "triangle trade." To be sure, immense wealth resulted: the countryside of England became dotted with elegant country houses paid for by the sale of slaves, their lives, and their labour. For investor, planter, and shipowner alike the trade was worth the effort. Less so was it evident that the European seamen like Roberts, who were sent to do the actual transport of slaves, shared in anything more than a brutal, hardscrabble existence that added the rigours of seamanship and the dangers of the sea to a coarsening, institutionalized cruelty in which human beings were reduced to the level of farm animals. Its toll on its practitioners was evident, in this description of slave-ship sailors released ashore as being of no further use:

> They were nightmarish in appearance. Some had the bruises, blotches, and bloody gums of scurvy. Some had burning ulcers caused by Guinea worms, which grew up to four feet long and festered beneath the skin of the lower legs and feet. Some had the shakes and sweats of malaria. Some had grotesquely swollen limbs and rotting toes. Some were blind, victims of a parasite … spread by black-flies in fast-flowing African rivers. Some had a starved and beaten appearance, courtesy of their captain.[12]

The ships themselves were little better, as the account of a contemporary eyewitness related:

> Stanfield was conscious of the sounds of the slave ship — the "long groan," "strain of anguish," cries, death songs, "shrieks of woe and howlings of despair!" All in this instance were heard in the midnight hour. Sickness was … part of the experience. Breathing "infected air" amid "green contagion," the fevered crew lie "strew'd o'er the filthy deck." Stanfield followed abolitionist surgeon Alexander Falconbridge in saying that the slave ship was "like a slaughterhouse. Blood, filth, misery, and disease."[13]

Even by the standards of a brutal age, the inducements that led men mostly in their twenties or younger — an average age in a slave-ship crew was twenty-six — to enter into the life of a slave-ship seaman are hard to see: a difficult existence akin to that of a merchant seaman, added to by the duties of prison guards. Several authors, as well as Rediker, shared the view that "slave-trade seamen came from numerous social backgrounds … but … as a whole were widely known as among the poorest occupational groups … the refuse and dregs of the Nation."[14]

In reading the memoirs of James Field Stanfield, a slave-ship sailor, one glimpses a spectrum of reasons why men entered the life, and the question begins to surface if any of these circumstances applied to Bartholomew Roberts. He certainly began poor, but somehow his path led to some education and betterment, and we have already mused on a possible naval experience for him. But what his path was remains tantalizingly unclear:

> By hook and by crook, a variety of people were lured aboard the ships. Some were drunk and indebted, forced to exchange a landed dungeon for a floating one. These included "restless youth" and those of "unwary mind," as well as those who thought they could outwit the crimp and ended up outwitting themselves. "Some few," wrote Stanfield, "the voluntary woe embrace." Some of these were smarting from "false friends"; some were feeling "undeserv'd disgrace"; some were no doubt in trouble with the law. Others had suffered misfortune of one kind or another, were "weary of griefs no passion can endure."
>
> Some had lost at love and were "of hopeless passion torn." Stanfield exemplified this last in a poem by a friend he called Russel, a "harmless spirit — gentlest of thy kind / Was ne'er to savage cruelty inclin'd." To the slave ship he was "by the winds and fiercer passions blown." Headed to the Tropics, he now "tries the ardours of the flaming zone." Slave-trade sailors were similar to those who sailed in other trades, but were perhaps a little more naïve, down and out, and desperate.[15]

To manage what in effect was a floating prison crammed full of suffering humanity, which had to be somehow navigated across a dangerous ocean with sufficient speed that enough of the "cargo" remained alive and marketable at its end, required of the ship's captain a kind of fatalistic ferocity. The contemporary writer "Dicky Sam" observed its effects, and these have been commented on by several historians, most effectively by Rediker:

> "Dicky Sam" described the violent reality of the slave ship this way: "the captain bullies the men, the men torture the slaves, the slaves' hearts are breaking with despair." The statement expresses an important truth. Violence cascaded downward, from captain and officers to sailors to the enslaved. Sailors, often beaten and abused themselves, took out their plight on the even more abject and powerless captives under their supervision and control. How this happened on any given ship would depend to a large extent on the captain, who had enormous latitude to run the ship as he wished. Even though captains and officers were the prime agents of disciplinary violence, sailors occupied the front line of social war on the ship.[16]

This grim assessment of what this meant as an environment in a slave ship for both crew and captives makes it surprising that anyone involved with the slave trade survived with any humanity at all, even given the casual brutality and cruelty of the age. Where on the spectrum of depravity Roberts's personality may have settled is difficult to see with clarity, as his career will show: an odd amalgam of order and even civility coexisting with a capacity for horrifying ruthlessness and barbarous punishment. Perhaps he was indeed a logical product of a cynical and brutalized business in a cynical and brutalized age, with sensitive — dare one even use the word *tender* — instincts crushed out of all recognition:

> [Slave-ship captains' power] in some inescapable measure depended on inflicting cruelty and suffering as a means of human control; it depended, in a word, on terror. This is

why hell, as a place of deliberately imposed torment, was such a good and useful analogy and in the end why abolitionists found it so easy to demonize the slave-ship captain in their propaganda. Not all masters of Guineamen were devils, but almost each and every one had the devil in him. This was not a flaw of individual personality or character. It was a requirement of the job and the larger economic system it served.[17]

"Had the devil in him." How telling an observation.

The slave ships that were collectively known as "Guineamen" were in some cases built for the trade, but for the most part converted from merchant vessels. The special requirements of transporting several hundred men, women, and children in farmyard conditions usually involved opening up the lower deck to provide a broad space, with low headroom, where the slaves could be penned down in long rows in dark misery, punctuated by visits to the "necessary" tubs provided for natural functions. The slaves would be released in batches onto the open weather deck for enough food, air, and exercise to keep them alive. Women were quartered separately from the men, and the whole prison area of the ship was blocked off from the slavers' part of the ship by a barricade, behind which the heavily armed crew could shelter in the event of a slave uprising. As it was in the slavers' interest to deliver as many slaves alive and in reasonable health as possible, the slaver captains avoided the use of heavy, plodding merchant ships, preferring instead relatively faster and handier vessels of smaller size, such as two-masted brigs. In later years of the trade, the fastest slavers were rakish American topsail schooners of a design that had come of age with the swift "Baltimore clippers" that sailed as privateers during the War of 1812. In Roberts's era in the early eighteenth century, the slaving brig or even a sloop was the most likely vessel to be found, and these vessels, as a rule, were smaller in size and cargo capacity than the full-rigged ships used by Europeans in the West Indian or East Indian trade. That smaller, nimble vessels were also preferred by pirates meant that a transition from slaver to pirate was never too difficult in a seamanship sense.[18]

It is perhaps fitting to grant Marcus Rediker the closing word on the nature and legacy of slave ships, and what they meant to the men who sailed them:

> The slave ship was a mobile, seagoing prison at a time when the modern prison had not yet been established on land. This truth was expressed in various ways at the time, not least because incarceration … was crucial to the slave trade. The ship itself was simply one link in a chain of enslavement. Stanfield called it a "floating dungeon," while an anonymous defender of the slave trade aptly called it a "portable prison." Liverpool sailors frequently noted that when they were sent to jail by tavern keepers for debt and from there bailed out by ship captains who paid their bills and took their labor, they simply exchanged one prison for another. And if the slave ship seemed a prison to a sailor, imagine how it seemed to a slave locked below decks for sixteen hours a day and more.[19]

To a degree, the use of physical force and violence, or the threat of it, that was required behaviour in most (but not all) slave ships meant that men inured to such things would not find the implicit violence of piracy that disturbing, in one view. Both pursuits involved inflicting pain or loss upon others. That reality may explain, partially, why so many men of slaving vessels readily accepted "recruitment" into the crews of pirate vessels when their ships were taken. As may become evident, the afloat society of a pirate vessel had much to recommend it — in the short term — to seamen enduring not only the casual harshness of the merchant seaman's work under dictatorial and often cruel captains, but also the prison guard existence required of a slaver that demanded indifference to human suffering. Both piracy and slavery were moving slowly from an accepted reality of European endeavour toward an anathema repugnant to that society; but that was not yet the case in 1718 when Roberts's *Princess* galley came under the guns of

Howell Davis's pirate vessel as it approached the West African coast on its mission of marketing suffering humanity.

The similar needs of pirates and slavers in the ships they employed — speed, handiness, simplicity of rig, and adaptability — made slavers good targets for pirates anxious to change or repair ships, and a "small ship" mentality was common to their approach to seamanship. If there was one employment at sea that would challenge fishing as the most desirable source of recruits for piracy's crews, it would prove to be the slave trade, with its hardened men inured to cruelty and the application of violence. It is to the ironically named "Sweet Trade" of the pirates that we now turn our attention.

3

The Sweet Trade

If there was one activity that challenged prostitution as one of the world's oldest professions, piracy would likely qualify. From the moment the first humans ventured out aboard even the most primitive of vessels, it was not long before others showed up on their own rafts or canoes to relieve them of their catch of fish or anything else worth stealing.

With no means to delineate territory on it, the sea remained into relatively modern times an uncontrolled theatre for banditry of all kinds. In the centuries before the rise of classical Greece, unnamed "sea peoples" raided the Egyptian coastline, and even with the rise of the Roman Empire, which turned the Mediterranean into *Mare Nostrum* — literally "our sea" — Roman shipping was plagued with piracy that declined only after pirate fleets were dealt crushing defeats by Roman war galleys. In Europe, through the Dark Ages, after the collapse of the Empire, until almost a thousand years later, Irish, Basque, Saxon, and Norse pirates preyed on coastal shipping and communities. With the seizure of the Levant in the 1400s by the Turks, Arab and Moorish pirates made the Mediterranean a hunting ground for their swift, lateen-rigged galleys.

It would not be until northern Europe recovered from the social catastrophes of the Reformation, the Counter-Reformation, and the Thirty Years War that the slow, steady growth of European nation-states and the establishment of their maritime power through national navies that the millennia of piracy in European waters came to an end. It would shift to the colonial waters opened by the discoveries of the 1400s and 1500s; waters where the European pirates found their last home, and suffered their final fate.

Piracy on the open ocean, as practised in the waters of the Caribbean, West Africa, and the Indian Ocean by principally British, French, and Dutch pirates, is considered to have taken place in three distinct active phases: one in the mid-1600s, a second from the late 1600s to about 1725, and a final, lesser period ending essentially with the Napoleonic Wars.

The middle period, from roughly the 1680s to the 1720s, is referred to by many as the "Golden Age of Piracy," for it was in that period that as many as four thousand mostly European pirates threatened to bring both Atlantic seaborne trade with the Americas and the slave trade from Africa to a halt. The end of the first phase of piracy, represented by the astonishing career of Henry Morgan, took place after 1670, when by the Treaty of Madrid, England and Spain agreed that peace in Europe should also mean peace in the lucrative West Indies, and a concerted effort to eradicate piracy began. Neither the peace nor that effort would last long, as the riches of the Americas flowing to Spain were too valuable a prize to resist. Nova Scotian historian Dan Conlin stated it succinctly:

> Gold and silver flowed in mind-boggling quantities from her vast conquered colonies on the American mainland, the fabled "Spanish Main." Spanish currency, such as gold doubloons and the silver dollars known as "Pieces of Eight," flooded the Atlantic world through illegal trade and buccaneering raids. Spanish money became the *de facto* world currency of the time.[1]

It is important to note that European pirates did not suddenly appear in towering vessels bristling with guns and manned by legions of desperate men armed to the teeth. The growth of what became known as the "Sweet Trade" was an evolution that passed through distinct stages. The origins lie in the bands of rootless men who roamed the forests of the island of Hispaniola and lived by hunting the wild pigs and cattle descended from those brought to the island by the Spanish a century before. Named *boucaniers* for their method of roasting and drying the meat over open fires on racks known as *boucains*, these rough, hardy men wore clothing of leather and lived a semi-wild lawless existence marked only by the excellence of their musketry with their exceptionally long guns: they had to be good shots to stay alive. Gradually, as the 1600s passed, the *boucaniers* — the term anglicized to *buccaneers* — began to supplement their rude existence by paddling out in dugout canoes and pouncing on unwary small vessels. In time they graduated from their canoes to the ships they captured, and began to develop a form of "home port" on the island of Tortuga, off Hispaniola's north coast. By the time Henry Morgan recruited many of them to take part in the 1671 attack on Panama, the buccaneers were still partly land brigands and partly sea bandits, though not in the sense of well-armed captains and crews able to challenge warships or merchant vessels on their own terms. Within a decade or so that would change as the pirates — best now to call them that — realized that a seagoing vessel had many advantages over a canoe, including the capacity to stay afloat, and began to haunt the bays and islands of the Caribbean. British, French, and Spanish preoccupation with the continuing state of quasi-war between them prevented governors and planters alike from moving from seeing these lawless men and their increasingly armed ships as useful providers of goods and services, to seeing them as a hindrance, and finally a threat. When a short-lived European peace took place in 1697, the British Board of Trade and the Admiralty finally crossed over to the decision that piracy could no longer be tolerated. Pirate historian Peter Earle portrays the decision clearly:

> Pirates were to be destroyed, not just as enemies of mankind but as enemies of capitalism and commercial expansion....
>
> [T]he pirates had a long innings ahead of them, but by the late 1720s these policies had been made effective.[2]

As Earle relates, it was timely that the Board of Trade and the Admiralty took this posture — even if they were ponderously slow to act on it —

41

because there came with the return of peace after the brief War of the League of Augsburg an "explosion of piracy on a scale never seen before."[3]

Britain was soon to be preoccupied with the resumption of the interminable war against Louis XIV, but the swarms of pirates already beginning to gather like flies around the Caribbean trade routes offered a chance to Britain to license them as privateers for the duration of the war. So as the century ended there were numerous small, well-armed craft packed with enterprising mariners who had a temporary sheen of legitimacy, which they would lose with the return of peace with the Treaty of Utrecht in 1713. The result of that was an immediate voiding of privateer licences and "letters of marque," and an upsurge in piracy, for complex reasons; as pirate historian David Cordingly explains:

> The second surge in piracy took place in the years following the Treaty of Utrecht in 1713 ... the size of the Royal Navy slumped from 53,785 in 1703 to 13,430 in 1715, putting 40,000 seamen out of work.... Many privateering commissions had been issued in the later years of the seventeenth century, particularly in the West Indies. Peace put an end to this, and the Governor of Jamaica warned London of the likely outcome: "Since the calling in of our privateers, I find already a considerable number of seafaring men at the towns of Port Royal and Kingston that can't find employment, who I am very apprehensive, for want of occupation in their way, may in a short time desert us and turn pirates."[4]

The governor's apprehension was well-placed, and in other maritime trades, pressures of economic downturn caused dissatisfaction in other "legitimate" pursuits, including the slave ships plying to West Africa. The conditions of life on those vessels in the first decades of the eighteenth century were such that mutinous reaction and a turn to piracy or other criminality was a constant threat.[5]

Historian Conlin provides the most succinct summary of the desperate conditions facing seamen at the end of the Louis XIV wars:

A vessel from the West Indies that had paid wartime wages of £4 a month in 1714 arrived in Lisbon and hired a new crew at a mere £1.15 a month.

Conditions for seamen grew worse as trade slumped by 1715. Many merchants and owners safeguarded their profits by, in the words of the sailors themselves, "using their men severely." They drove their men hard, cheated them of wages and shortchanged their rations. The life of a sailor, always hard and dangerous, was now bleak, grinding and often hopeless.[6]

That profits could still be pursued by merchants and investors in this labour-rich atmosphere was clear, and the profitable new reasons for the continuation of the slave trade, even with the opportunity to have no regard for the welfare of the men who made it all work, were clear, as Marcus Rediker points out:

> The end of the War of Spanish Succession [in 1713] brought a rich and shiny prize for British merchants: the *Asiento*, which gave these traders the legal right to ship forty-eight hundred slaves a year, and the illegal right to ship many more, to Spanish America through the South Sea Company. This incentive, coupled with [deregulation] of the African slave trade in 1712 ... dramatically increased the importance of the slave trade in the eyes of British merchants and the state.[7]

Overall, it is not difficult to see the motivations of harassed or poorly treated seamen who were at the bottom level of a social ladder of vast unfairness, one that led to those riches and privileges they were forever to be denied access even though their labour made them possible. Before their eyes, as governments or merchants either mistreated them or discarded them as useless if sick or injured, a panorama of expanding wealth unfolded after 1713 that may have simply proven too hard to resist. The scale of the lure was enormous, as historian Douglas Botting reveals:

There were Spanish treasure fleets laden with the priceless produce of the gold and silver mines of Spanish America; convoys of Portuguese merchantmen stuffed with the riches of Brazil; an endless stream of cargo boats shipping out the exports of the North American colonies to England; the ships of the Royal Africa Company and other European charter companies bringing out gold and ivory and slaves from the interior of West Africa; the Mecca pilgrim ships and the merchant fleets of the Grand Mogul of India carrying gold, precious stones and luxury goods between the Red Sea, the Persian Gulf, and the mainland of India; the magnificent East Indiamen, blown by the monsoons across the Indian Ocean and round the Cape with their holds full of silks and jewels, spices and muslins acquired by the East India companies established along the Indian coasts ... [s]uch were the prizes.[8]

Intermittently, war would cloud the scene again, as in 1718 to 1720, but for the thousands of pirates at sea in those years, naval forces had yet to become a serious threat. That would change dramatically. But, for the moment, to the pirate crews feasting on helpless merchantmen, all the sea was a hunting ground, and one is reminded of, in another context, the words of Étienne de Flacourt, governor of Madagascar, who in 1658 observed about the 1494 Treaty of Tordesillas, which optimistically drew a line to divide the ocean world between Spain and Portugal: "Beyond the line, there are no more friends and anything afloat is a prize."[9] And indeed that was the case.

For the common seaman, life on the lawless seas in the merchant service or in a naval warship was still a precarious business, threatened as it was by the dangers of life at sea, disease and injury as we have seen, and the reality that "it was not unusual for a seaman to say good-bye to his family and not see them again for months and sometimes years."[10]

In many cases the sailor had little in the way of permanent roots ashore, and as Rediker has pointed out, usually came from the lowest social classes, was poor, and before going to sea had been employed in the meanest and most shadowy of shore occupations. In many cases, orphans and foundlings from the British underclass were the source. They were often as not considered, "as a royal official condescendingly observed, 'desperate Rogues' who could have little hope in life ashore."[11] The sailor was decades away from being the romanticized, sturdy guardian of Britain's society, the "jolly tar" of William Boyce's anthem "Heart of Oak."

The picture begins to form of men who, aware even if dimly of their hopeless place at the bottom of the eighteenth-century pyramid of social privilege, led lives of prevailing hardship and a degree of uncertainty almost impossible for the modern mind to grasp. With the wit to understand that they mattered little to the world other than as expendable labour, it took very little to have them give up convention and become, in their own words, "at war with all the world."[12] Life offered little encouragement to the contrary.

Such men, who had essentially given up hope, were ready to become, as Earle notes, "the men of no country, the men of the sea *sans foi et sans aveu*"[13] ("without faith and without confession"), which is how pirates came to view themselves. That they constituted a serious threat to the established order was not lost on members of the privileged sectors of society: Edmund Dummer, who established the first Caribbean mail service, remarked that after 1713 "it is the opinion of everyone this cursed trade [privateering] will breed so many pirates that when peace comes, we shall be in more danger from them than we are now from the enemy."[14] Prescient words, indeed.

It would be fair to say that the iniquities of seventeenth and eighteenth century European society, still many decades away from the great social shattering of the French Revolution and the Napoleonic era, were at the base of why men, who might have acted differently if allowed social mobility, were drawn to the brief, incandescent finality of piracy. As another of Roberts's biographers, Stanley Richards, noted scathingly:

> All the inducements were toward making pirates. Moral deterrents were practically non-existent, for dishonesty was rampant in all strata of society. The wealthy and powerful cornered money with fanatical zeal — it was a

case of the end justifying the means. Thus a Treasurer of the Navy, the Earl of Anglesey, plundered the Chatham Chest (which contained funds for relieving a modicum of the distress of aged and disabled sailors) of thousands of pounds. He was not brought to book. The poor had no real right to anything except hard work, starvation, and a pauper's grave when death claimed them. The laws were made by the rich who used them as a cover to exploit the common people. Then when the starving stole to live, the laws framed by the powerful hanged them. But no law seemed to overtake the rich.[15]

Though individuals were known to have been drawn to piracy as an escape from life ashore, the overwhelming majority of pirates were seamen, and many were merchant seamen who had been captured and then volunteered.[16]

Subsequent research has revealed that there were two principal recruiting sources for the pirate crews after 1713, as Earle explains succinctly:

[T]here were two trades which stood out as a source of willing men. The first was the Newfoundland fishery which attracted the pirates of the 1710s just as it had those of a century earlier. Here every summer there were some two thousand English and American sailors and fishermen, "shamefully exploited by the masters of their ships" and doing work of "extraordinary labour and pains," perfect recruits for the pirate ships who came to Newfoundland "to get better manned." The West African slave trade was an even better recruiting ground for pirates, the crews of slavers being "generally glad of an opportunity of entering with them."[17]

It would take years of experience in the naval wars of the eighteenth century, well after the bloody end of the "Golden Age of Piracy" in the 1720s, for realization to begin to set in that brutality and unfairness in the management of men at sea needed changing. Admiral Edward Vernon, writing during the reign of George II, offered not only that the navy's fleet was "manned by violence and maintained by cruelty," but that "the readiest way [to man the ships] will be to endeavour to regain their affections by a more humane treatment for the future."[18] It was a lesson not to be learned until well after the pirate scourge had been bloodily swept from the seas.

In the period of greatest pirate activity, roughly 1715 to 1725, there were essentially three types of pirates: there were the men little different from the *boucaniers* of the seventeenth century, who set out from Caribbean beaches and coves as ships passed, with dugout canoes or longboats, to make their attacks; the Bahamas and the Virgin Islands had become home to a more ambitious type of pirate, who manned small, handy, single-mast sloops able to overtake and pounce on ships passing near their haunts; and, lastly, the heavily armed open-ocean pirate such as Bartholomew Roberts, manning powerful full-rigged ships with many guns and fully capable of taking on an armed merchantman — or many naval vessels for that matter — and who sailed the waters of West Africa, the Indian Ocean, the West Indies, and the North American coasts as far north as Newfoundland. This last category posed the greatest threat to oceangoing trade, whether in goods or the living cargos of slaves.

The physical appearance of pirates rarely approached the bejewelled and sashed look so beloved of later artists, who lent an air of romance to the very unromantic "Sweet Trade." For the most part, pirates looked very much like the common merchant seamen they mostly had been, perhaps a bit more ragged until a capture allowed a "shift of clothes," but still distinct from landsmen. As David Cordingly wrote, sailors simply "looked different; their faces and arms were burnt and weathered to [a] nut-brown colour … [t]hey were liable to have scars and injuries from handling sails and gear in heavy weather," and above all they were distinguished by their clothes:

In the early years of the eighteenth century most landsmen wore long coats and long waistcoats over knee breeches and stockings. Seamen on the other hand wore short [often] blue jackets, over a checked shirt, and either long canvas trousers or baggy "petticoat breeches," which somewhat resembled culottes. In addition, they frequently wore red waistcoats, and tied a scarf or handkerchief loosely around the neck.[19]

Pirates were mostly young men in their midtwenties, which Cordingly reports "was exactly the same as the average age of a merchant seaman ... and similar to the average of seamen in the Royal Navy." He goes on to point out that the youthfulness of the crews was largely due to the physical demands of working a ship at sea in all weather: agility, fitness, stamina, a certain amount of physical strength, and a capacity to endure extreme discomfort. The average pirate — and the men he preyed on — was an immensely tough, hardy individual who came by his disdain for landsmen honestly, for his school of experience was beyond anything faced ashore save by miners. The open ocean was his to command and roam if he survived its perils, both human and natural. In the pirate community, the pirate found men of similar experience, but a freedom from the strictures of lawful society was a heady thing to experience when first encountered. As Rediker explained, sailors came to pirate ships after working on merchant and naval ships, where they suffered poor working conditions, brutal discipline, and low pay. Piracy offered "the prospect of plunder and 'ready money,' abundant food and drink ... and joyous camaraderie, all as expressions of an ethic of justice."[20]

The sense of release was intoxicating. As one pirate recalled, "we might sing, sweare, drab [whore], and kill men as freely as your cakemakers do flies ... when the whole sea was our empire where we robbed at will."[21]

It was typical of a pirate vessel of the third, ocean-capable category that it routinely carried far more men than comparable merchantmen. Cordingly relates that a merchant vessel of a hundred tons burthen could carry perhaps twelve men, but a pirate vessel of the same size might carry eighty or more, to handle the ship's sails and sweeps and man the ship's guns. With such close proximity and denied ready access to women ashore, authors have raised the question of widespread homosexuality being practised among pirates. Cordingly replies:

The fact is that the vast majority of seamen, when not actively engaged in working the ship, seem to have spent far more time thinking about women than about men. They wrote letters to women, they sang sea chanties and ballads about women, they tattooed their bodies with the names of women, they scratched pictures of women on whales' teeth and walrus tusks, they collected souvenirs ... to take back to [them], and they treasured mementos from the women they had left behind at home. And they thought about their women when they went into battle.[22]

Where there seems little controversy is in the issue of pirates' drinking habits, and the almost biblical importance of rum in their lives. Even by the standards of the eighteenth century, pirates were observed to be drunk as often as possible and drunk all the time if practical. The final demise of Bartholomew Roberts was possibly the result of heavy intoxication among his crew as the Royal Navy closed in on them. Given the tendency of water casks to go foul shortly after a vessel got out to sea, the practice of drinking "small beer" and spirits or wine was common in all ships of the era. Pirates, however, lifted drinking to an entirely new level of accomplishment. Cordingly explains its significance:

All seamen were notorious for their drinking habits. Marcus Rediker has pointed out that seamen drank for a variety of reasons: because good drink was easier to find on a ship than good victuals and fortified them against the cold and wet; because drink enabled them to forget the rigors of shipboard life for a while; and because drinking performed a valuable social function. Seamen drank together to relax, to celebrate, to gossip and get to know each other. During meals they drank toasts to their wives and mistresses, to the King, to a successful voyage.[23]

Pirates did indeed toast the King, surprisingly: their argument tended to be with everyone below him in the social order. Pirates added to the above list of justifications a declaration of freedom from the strictures of society or the heavy hand of a merchant captain by unlimited drinking, and few pirate captains attempted to use their limited authority to deny a man a drink: it led too often to an unsheathed blade or a cocked pistol. There was little about the pirate life to complain about — except perhaps its brevity — and much to attract young, active men without hope of betterment elsewhere: "[T]here was the pirate round, which ensured that the ship always sailed in pleasant weather, the camaraderie, the freedom from irksome discipline, the informality ... and, not to be forgotten, the chance of booty."[24]

The so-called pirate round was a migration each year made possible by the prodigious open-ocean seamanship and navigation of captains like Bartholomew Roberts and others of his skill level. As Earle outlines,

> [They sailed] out of the West Indies in the early summer and up the American coast as far as Newfoundland from where, like the pirates based in Ireland a century earlier, they sailed south to avoid the northern winter.... [Their goal] would normally be the Leeward Islands and Barbados where the pirates lay in wait for the provision ships which arrived around Christmas. And from there, in later years, they would sail to Africa, Brazil and the Indian Ocean, some of them coming back to the West Indies to start the round all over again.[25]

A substantial pirate community established itself for a time on the island of Madagascar, preying on both European ships voyaging into the Indian Ocean, and Indian and Arab ships.

If there was one characteristic of these able mariners that marked them, it was their preoccupation with weapons: pistols, dirks, cutlasses, boarding axes, and other bizarre weaponry. As artist and historian William Gilkerson observes, weaponry was central to a pirate's image of himself:

> [M]any pirates nurtured their reputations as fierce combatants at close quarters and cultivated ferocious images by hanging weapons everywhere about their persons, like walking arsenals: a pirate could have as many arms as he could wear and keep clean, for in that society, cleanliness of one's weaponry sometimes substituted for godliness.[26]

Even given their proclivity for drink and dangerous displays of weaponry — presumably not when they were sail-handling aboard ship at sea — pirates were not blind to the fact that organization and a degree of subordination and responsibility were required to take a vessel to sea safely. They had escaped the lawful world through a rejection of authority, but soon built a tradition of their own, a kind of egalitarian sharing of responsibility that became known as the "Jamaica Discipline." In an age when democratic egalitarianism was barely conceived of in modern terms, pirate societies established themselves as reasonably equal societies in which each man had a vote, the senior positions of captain and quartermaster were selected — in many cases, but by no means universally — by crew vote, and the ship's course and destination were also arrived at by vote. There were exceptions to all this; a number of pirate captains simply continued in charge of ships they had previously commanded legally, and brooked little dissent. But Bartholomew Roberts would be one who fit the classic mould: elected by his crew, and holding that office at their whim. It was unheard-of democracy, in a sense, and it is remarkable that pirates managed to make their miniature societies work on that basis even while they recognized that the sea demanded little concern for politics but a great deal about survival. As a result, as Cordingly observes, "pirate life at sea was well organized, and similar in many respects to life on a merchant ship ... ocean voyaging demanded a certain level of discipline if the crew were going to survive the perils of the sea."[27]

Bartholomew Roberts rose to command his ship, as we will see, by vote of the crew. But a pirate captaincy was not the fearsome exercise of autocracy that held in the navy or the merchant service. In the egalitarian spirit of pirate society, Roberts, as captain, "was allowed the use of the master's cabin, and a small amount of silver cutlery and china crockery. But this meant little. At any hour of the day or night a crewman could enter the cabin and help himself to Roberts' food and drink."[28]

Somehow, these strange republics of shaggy ruffians managed at the same time to institute the same offices and functions that warships or merchantmen had: gunners, gunner's mates, carpenters, boatswain, sailmakers, and so on. All had their roles in the pirate ship, governed by often ad hoc terms of agreement. As Rediker observes, "the early-eighteenth-century pirate ship was a world turned upside down, made so by the articles of agreement that established the rules and customs of the pirates' alternative social order. Pirates 'distributed justice,' elected their officers, divided their loot equally, and established a different discipline."[29]

The most complete agreement made by pirates to allow them to survive the sea and each other was that drafted by Bartholomew Roberts, stung after an underling, Walter Kennedy, made off with his ship and most of a recently acquired haul of booty while Roberts was distracted, in direct contravention of the "all for one, one for all" ethos that pirates themselves valued. Roberts had his surviving crew swear to these new articles on a Bible, and they helped in his subsequent assembly of so potent a piratical fighting force that it took an all-out effort by the Royal Navy to defeat it. The "Articles" provided, in essence, as follows:

1. Every man shall have an equal vote in affairs of moment. He shall have an equal title to the fresh provisions or strong liquors at any time seized, and shall use them at pleasure unless a scarcity may make it necessary for the common good that a retrenchment may be voted.
2. Every man shall be called fairly in turn by the list on board of prizes, because over and above their proper share, they are allowed a shift of clothes. But if they defraud the company to the value of even one dollar in plate, jewels or money, they shall be marooned. If any man rob another he shall have his nose and ears slit, and be put ashore where he shall be sure to encounter hardships.

3. None shall game for money either with dice or cards.

4. The lights and candles should be put out at eight at night, and if any of the crew desire to drink after that hour they shall sit upon the open deck without lights.

5. Each man shall keep his piece, cutlass, and pistols at all times clean and ready for action.

6. No boy or woman to be allowed amongst them. If any man shall be found seducing any of the latter sex and carrying her to sea in disguise he shall suffer death.

7. He that shall desert the ship or his quarters in time of battle shall be punished by death or marooning.

8. None shall strike another on board the ship, but every man's quarrel shall be ended on shore by sword or pistol in this manner. At the word of command from the quartermaster, each man being previously placed back to back, at so many paces distance, shall turn and fire immediately. If any man do not, the quartermaster shall knock the piece out of his hand. If both miss their aim they shall take to their cutlasses, and he that draws the first blood shall be declared the victor.

9. No man shall talk of breaking up their way of living till each has a share of £1,000. Every man who shall become a cripple or lose a limb in the service shall have 800 dollars from the common stock and for lesser hurts proportionally.

10. The captain and the quartermaster shall each receive two shares of a prize, the master, boatswain, and gunner, one share and a half, and other officers, one and one quarter.

11. The musicians shall have rest on the Sabbath Day only by right. On all other days by favour only.[30]

To a degree this was a remarkable document, and historians with a good deal of idealism see in it a precursor of declarations of independence or social justice that would appear almost a century later in America and France. The likelihood is that it was simply a common-sense document designed to keep violent men who knew they had no hope of advancement in the world left from tearing each other apart, and hastening their doom at the gibbet, the receiving end of a naval broadside, or the always-appalling dangers of open-ocean sailing. Anyone who has been to sea in a traditional-rig vessel, knows it is a place for endurance, teamwork, personal responsibility, and a level head, and from documents like these comes a clear picture that the desperate or resigned men who took to piracy often lacked both literacy and a basic knowledge of the challenging arts of transoceanic ship navigation, even in the days of "log, latitude and lookout," a half-century before longitude could be determined. To survive, the pirates had to have a degree of order and observable rules, and in that they were cut essentially from the same cloth as the men who pursued them. The story of piracy, Earle submits,

> is the story of two sets of predators, one composed of pirates chasing merchant shipping and the other of men of the navy chasing pirates. Both groups of men were ironically drawn from the same milieu and had many customs and skills in common, for both were what contemporaries called 'bred to the sea,' men whose early maritime training had been acquired mainly in merchant shipping.[31]

In essence, Earle would have us believe there was little to choose between the Royal Navy seaman and the pirate who was his prey; the same vices, the same skills, the same unique character of the "tall ship" sailor. The only important differences were that "the pirates had freer access to drink and the navy had discipline on its side and so the naval vessels usually won on those rare occasions when they brought a pirate ship to battle."[32]

The pirate had found a home in the ship's company of mates with whom he had cut the last bonds of obligation, duty, and acquiescence to the ordered, lawful world. He was already a dead man, and he knew it, for the numbers of men out of the thousands who turned pirate that survived with enough money to escape and fund a life ashore was almost negligible. Yet in his rum-soaked haze and brandishing his many pistols, he had a last, remaining loyalty, and that was to the coarse, rough-hewn society of equally doomed men with whom he had cast his lot. Even when general pardons were offered, as the British Crown offered in 1717, they were largely ignored. Pirates were caught in the "Sweet Trade" by circumstance and finally by liking: being "from the seas," as they replied when asked what country they hailed from, was more apt than they realized. The noted English wit and writer Samuel Johnson (1709–1784), who had never been a sailor, once cleverly if inaccurately observed: "No man will be a sailor who has contrivance enough to get himself into a jail; for being in a ship is being in jail with the chance of being drowned.... A man in jail has more room, better food, and commonly better company."[33]

For the sea-hardened "lost" men of the pirate community, nothing could have been farther from the truth. And it was into this society that Bartholomew Roberts would be thrust.

4

Piracy and Canada

Pirates were attracted to the rich fishing grounds off Newfoundland less for the money carried by large Grand Banks fishing vessels, which was modest, than for the ample supplies they had aboard, and especially for their men themselves. This was an ideal hunting ground for manpower.[1]

Writing in 2009, this writer's efforts to expand the knowledge of piracy in Canada began with a challenge to the enduring myth about pirates' exploits that they carried out their foul deeds only under waving palms, and off gleaming sand beaches or the coral lagoons of the tropics. Staying alive was easier in the warmer climes of the south, although mosquito-borne fevers might carry off most of a crew in a few days, but there was booty and swag to be had in the cold waters of the north as well, and the lure of that sort of wealth brought its share of pirates to the waters of what would become Canada.

A principal lure for northern pirates, as we have already seen, was the huge industry surrounding the Grand Banks fishery, in place since the 1470s and now led by the British, French, and Portuguese, the Spanish being busy plundering South America of its seemingly inexhaustible treasure. The North American fishery required some ten thousand men and over four hundred well-equipped ships, as well as shore stations to support the visiting fleets, particularly the English, who dried their catch onshore rather than carrying it home whole, as the Portuguese and others did. The fleets that congregated each year on the Newfoundland, Nova Scotia, and Labrador coasts were governed by no authority other than that of the first captain to arrive each year, who was given the title of fishing admiral. With hordes of seamen to prey upon as potential additions to a pirate crew, and with ships and shore stations brimming with equipment, supplies, gear, and the services of shipwrights and men skilled in all the seagoing trades, the fishery became a rich prize that the pirate brethren could not resist, particularly off Newfoundland. And if the pickings in the fishery were lean, the great convoys of the plate fleets sailing their ponderous way home to Spain from Havana passed a mere three hundred miles to the south. This flame soon attracted the black-flagged pirate moths. And a rum and desperate lot they were, as we have seen.

Remarkably, few true pirates were put to sea from the ports of Acadia or New France to prey on the shipping of local waters. Bureaucratic control over who went to sea to do what, and the reality that piracy committed in home waters is a risky business at best, meant that most armed French vessels in Canadian waters that were not part of *la marine royale* were licensed privateers. European French privateers, and more than a few from New France, preferred the pickings of the Caribbean, the Indian Ocean, and the wealthy, ill-defended towns and shipping of colonial Spanish America. Still, a number of New France or Acadian seamen did enter the notoriety of open-Atlantic piracy, among them Pierre Maisonnat (dit Baptiste), and an unlucky individual known as Pierre le Picard.

Le Picard's origins are not recorded, but it is likely that he was an *acadien*. Le Picard heaves into view in 1667, when he is listed as a crewman in a brigantine commanded by the Frenchman Francois L'Ollonais, which was cruising in the Caribbean. L'Ollonais, who had a reputation for sadistic cruelty, was intending to raid the coast of Nicaragua but was blown off course to Honduras. Undeterred, he sacked the town of San Pedro de Puerto Caballos, then waited three months to attack a reputed treasure galleon, only to find that it carried no bullion. Le Picard left L'Ollonais at this point with a few followers, determined to march overland to the town of Panama as Henry Morgan had done in 1671. Le Picard was no Morgan, and the Spanish repelled his little band with ease.

Afterward, Le Picard appears here and there around the Caribbean in varying and mostly unsuccessful raids on small towns and ports. Having earned little but adventure stories from his wanderings, he appears to have returned to Acadia to settle around 1690. He went to sea once more during the time of the William Phips's attacks on Acadia, during which he apparently took part in a privateering raid on the coast of Rhode Island. The success of this venture is unknown.

Newfoundland waters, where Bartholomew Roberts would come to full flower as a pirate leader, continued to be the great northern magnet for piracy, or for privateering attacks that bordered on piracy. The first true pirate worthy of the name to inflict himself on Newfoundland was the handsome and aristocratic Peter Easton, who arrived in St. John's Harbour in 1611 with no fewer than ten ships bristling with armament, including his own flagship, the 350-ton *Happy Adventure*. Easton demanded that the local fishing admiral, Richard Whitbourne, provide him with five hundred fishermen and supplies with which to attack Spanish shipping, particularly the treasure fleets crossing from the West Indies to Spain by the northern Atlantic route. That Spain and England were officially at peace was not lost on Whitbourne, who nonetheless yielded to Easton's superior manner and air of entitlement — not to forget his guns. Easton got 1,500 men and enough supplies to establish a fortified base for himself at Harbour Grace.

Easton was not without his nerve. Secretly bankrolled by the Killigrew family of Pendennis Castle, Cornwall, Easton had built a lucrative trade in bold piracy in the English Channel and coastal Europe until, by 1610, he commanded a formidable squadron of forty ships. King James, the din of protesting merchants ringing in his ears, finally appointed an aristocratic lawyer and opportunist, Henry Mainwaring, to assemble a fleet and put an end to Easton's depredations. Hearing of this, Easton took his best ships and fled south to the coast of West Africa for a year's profitable, if unhealthy, cruising before deciding that it was safe to re-establish himself in Newfoundland.

Having secured Whitbourne's grudging co-operation, Easton finished at Harbour Grace, a well-provided shore station featuring a small, solid fort and the stockpiled lootings from twenty-five French, twelve

Portuguese, and one unlucky Flemish vessel, in addition to a hefty arsenal of one hundred captured guns. Once his fleet had been thoroughly readied, and with a watchful garrison left behind in the bristling fort, Easton sailed off to the tropic delights of Puerto Rico, where he captured not only El Morro Castle, the guardian of San Juan harbour, but the treasure galleon *San Sebastien*, which was about to depart for Spain. Easton's loot-packed ships wallowed back to Harbour Grace only to find a fleet of Basque ships, fresh from capturing his fort and station, sailing out to do battle. Easton was in no mood for half measures, and in the ferocious battle that ensued every single Basque ship was sunk, captured, or run aground.

Now with undisputed mastery of the coast, Easton built a personal "retreat" at Ferryland, while still maintaining his operational base at Harbour Grace. This period, 1612 to 1614, was the high point of his piratical career, and he capped it by sailing with his fleet to the vicinity of the Azores Islands, where, consistent with his extraordinary luck, he captured the Spain-bound treasure fleet and sailed home to Harbour Grace with his ships almost awash with the weight of the spectacular plunder.

A fight between a pirate vessel like the ones in Easton's fleet and a Spanish plate galleon or Basque fisherman was a fearsome process, made deliberately so by the pirate fighting methods, which would hold in Roberts's later day as it did in Easton's. The preferred pirate vessel was a single-masted sloop, a light, handy, and swift craft that could easily sail away from trouble if the prey proved too stubborn to capture or danger approached in the form of a pursuing warship. Easton, however, commanded a heterogeneous fleet that included heavily armed, full-rigged ships that were the equal of Crown warships. As in those naval warships, Easton's crews were notoriously overcrowded into their vessels, with many men being carried to simultaneously sail and "fight" the ship, and to overwhelm their opponents in the savage work of hand-to-hand fighting after boarding.

A pirate vessel approaching for the attack was a frightening sight indeed. The pirate usually tried for the "windward gauge," the position upwind of the prey that allowed the pirate to run down at will for the attack or sheer off if the defence seemed too stalwart. The deck of the vessel would be crammed with noisy pirates who often delighted in adding outlandish additions to their normally drab and often ragged merchant seamen's clothing. Frequently, they blackened their faces to affect a more threatening air. In their delight with weapons they frequently staggered about the deck overladen with dirks, cutlasses, boarding axes, pikes, and braces of long flintlock pistols, sometimes hung about them on ribbon lanyards for easy use.

As the pirate vessel rushed in for the attack — providing the terror-stricken victim had not simply and quickly surrendered — aloft it would be flying huge, oversized banners and flags, not only of England or other nations, but ones emblazoned with threatening designs and in either the traditional black or the dreaded red of the flag of no quarter — the *jolie rouge* or Jolly Roger that meant slaughter to all who resisted. The pirates on deck not handling lines would be baying out dreadful threats and curses to overawe their victims, and, in an incongruous touch, any musicians on board would be gathered somewhere on deck, blaring out drum-heavy anthems and fanfares that added to the general nightmar-ishness of the spectacle. All this was calculated: surrender without a fight was what most pirates wanted, as we have seen — damaged ships and goods were of little value — and those who did not resist were usually plundered but not harmed. It was a different matter for those crews who fought back, for the pirates were merciless if opposed — Roberts among them — and some were psychotics and sadists, who killed or tortured even the meekest of victims.

Boarding was the preferred method of taking a prize, as we have noted in our look at the "Sweet Trade." It avoided damage and brought the numbers and fighting skills of the pirates into play. Surging in from windward, the pirate vessel's whipstaff (a vertical lever that controls the ship's rudder) would be put "hard over" and the hulls would crash together, grapnels flying across the leaping foam between the ships, and the boarders would launch themselves over the rail of the victim with a collective roar in their throats and the gleam of booty in their eyes. Rare was the opponent vessel that successfully resisted such an attack. More often, the pirate ship would range up alongside the quarry and invite its captain over for a chat about the good sense of surrendering easily — an argument usually won quickly.

As Easton's Newfoundland fort rang with the roar and clink of rum-drenched celebration, the somewhat tardy arm of the Crown in the form of Henry Mainwaring was closing in, albeit slowly, on the pirates. Learning of Mainwaring's approach, Easton sped off a note to James I, supported by appropriate gifts, requesting a pardon.

In timely fashion and obviously through good seamanship on the part of the dispatch vessel, the pardon arrived before Mainwaring's fleet did, and Easton paid off his crews in handsome fashion before sailing off alone to the Mediterranean, a pardoned and extremely wealthy man. There he concluded a deal with the Duke of Savoy that allowed Easton to buy a beautiful estate by the sea, title himself Marquis of Savoy and Master of Ordnance for the Duke, and live a lengthy life in supreme luxury, perhaps the most fortunate pirate of all.

The man sent in pursuit of Easton was cut from much the same cloth of aristocratic entitlement and scant regard for the law. Henry Mainwaring was but twenty-four when in 1610 he received the commission to hunt down Easton, or at least put a stop to his flagrant piracy in the English Channel. Easton duly hustled off to Newfoundland on the news, but Mainwaring was not one to miss a main chance. Convincing the king to grant him a privateering commission to attack Spanish ships outside European waters, Mainwaring spent two leisurely years enriching himself and his crews by attacking Spanish shipping off Africa's slave ports, before finally sailing off to Newfoundland in pursuit of Easton, if *pursuit* is the right word.

Arriving at St. John's, Mainwaring cornered the hapless Whitbourne — again the fishing admiral, by his ill luck — and used the privateering licence to demand stores and men from the fishing fleet. Mainwaring occupied Easton's fort and buildings at Harbour Grace, plundered any Spanish or Portuguese vessels within reach, then sailed off to the West African coast to take his turn preying on Spanish shipping.

When King James received complaints from the Spanish, he ignored them, so the Spanish assembled a fleet, which fell on Mainwaring's own fleet as it passed Portugal on its way to England. Mainwaring shattered the Spanish, to their enormous chagrin, and pleased James so much he commissioned Mainwaring into the Royal Navy, gave him command of

Dover Castle, and knighted him. He would rise eventually to become Vice-Admiral Sir Henry Mainwaring, a career that was aided immeasurably by some cash-heavy gifts to the king at key moments.

Easton and Mainwaring are large, almost fictional-seeming characters in the history of eastern Canadian waters. But there were many minor figures who were carried along on the same course of plunder, and several are worth particular notice.

One whose story has yet to be fully told is beautiful Sheila NaGeira, so-called Pirate Queen of the Newfoundland coast. The girl's real name was Sheila O'Connor, and she had been taken prisoner by a Dutch privateer, where her beauty both made her a great prize and put her at great risk. In a savage mid-Atlantic battle, one of Peter Easton's ships defeated the Dutch privateer and O'Connor found herself with Easton's band. Sharing in their freebooting adventures, she finally fell in love with one of Easton's lieutenants, Gilbert Pike. Together with Pike, she left Easton's service when the latter sailed off to Savoy, and with their share of the payout they set up a fishing station and seamen's tavern at Mosquito, which is now Bristol's Hope on Conception Bay. For years after, it was rumoured that unmarked longboats rowed out of hidden coves with pirate crews led by a beautiful woman, and plundered vessels of the anchored fishing fleets. Her story has never been fully revealed.

Pirates had their share of murderous psychotics in their ranks, and one of these was Edward Low. Low had become a pirate in the eighteenth-century Caribbean after losing his wife and child in New England in tragic circumstances that pushed him into madness, biographers claim. Having come north with his sloop and crew to harass New England shipping, he was pursued by a Massachusetts provincial warship sent out from Boston to find him. Low eluded the Massachusetts vessel by abandoning his ship after capturing another, and sailed off with the latter into Nova Scotian waters.

Rounding into Roseway Harbour near Shelburne, Low captured no fewer than thirteen fishing vessels, taking one for his new flagship, which he named the *Fancy*. Releasing the fishermen to sail home in his former ship, Low sailed northeast along the Nova Scotia coast, then crossed to the south coast of Newfoundland.

Working round to St. John's, he peered in through the rocky gates of the harbour and spotted what appeared to be a substantial merchant ship. When Low sailed in to attack the anchored vessel, it opened up a thunderous broadside — the ship was a naval frigate — that sent Low hustling out to sea. Furious at this rebuff, Low looted a settlement near Carbonear with almost gleeful brutality and then took eight Grand Banks vessels in quick succession before fleeing south to warmer climes for the winter.

Somehow surviving a hurricane, the *Fancy* cruised the Spanish Main, then crossed to the West African coast, with Low's cruel treatment of his captives building an even greater demonic reputation for him. With the *Fancy* laden with bullion and other plunder, Low returned to North American waters in the fall of 1723, sailing quietly up into the Bay of Fundy.

A number of sources claim that Low and his crew dragged chests of treasure ashore on high, cliff-faced Isle Haute and buried them there, confident that Fundy's dangerous tides and the remoteness of the island would keep the stash safe. Sailing south out of Fundy, Low began to act with such maniacal cruelty and sadism toward the crews and passengers of captured ships that his sickened crew finally put him over the side in a small boat with three other men and sailed away. A short time later Low was found by a French warship and taken to Martinique, where the French lost no time in stringing him up to a gibbet. The vast hoard he allegedly left on Isle Haute, far to the north, has never been found.

Among a number of pirates who found Canada's waters as rich a hunting ground as the Caribbean was a rare piratical man-and-wife team, Eric Cobham and Maria Lindsey. Cobham had stolen money at an inn in Oxford, England, early in the eighteenth century — for which the innocent innkeeper was hanged — and used it to buy a small armed vessel at Plymouth. Enlisting a particularly murderous crew, he put to sea and fell upon a returning East Indiaman in the Irish Sea. After emptying the ship of a priceless cargo, Cobham sank the vessel, with all its crew sealed below, before sailing off to sell his loot in the unquestioning marketplace of the French Mediterranean coast. Returning to Plymouth, he fell in with a woman who equalled him in ruthlessness, Maria Lindsey. Together, the two embarked on a marital career of piracy, their first joint victim being an American vessel taken off Nantucket shortly after the Cobhams arrived in those waters. They continued with their policy that "dead men tell no tales," and were it not for their own recollections, their depredations would never have come to light, due to their expedient (unlike most pirates) of killing everyone on board any vessel they took and sinking it — to be presumed "lost at sea" — after unloading what they wished of the cargo.

The Cobhams found that Cabot Strait, between Newfoundland and Cape Breton Island, was a highway for French ships laden with goods and money steering for Quebec, and others laden with furs outbound for France. Scouting the innumerable coves of the Newfoundland coast, the Cobhams set up a fortified base at Sandy Point, on Bay St. George. From there, they swept out in all seasons to prowl their hunting grounds of the Strait, the Gulf, and the shores of Isle Saint-Jean (later Prince Edward Island). In their extraordinary twenty-year career, their activities were never suspected, their base at Sandy Point never attacked, all as a result of their unhesitating murder of all and any they came upon. Their careers ended when they retired to the coast of France, living near Le Havre in respected comfort — he even became a magistrate — until Maria committed suicide. Cobham died in his bed, having earlier confessed their life story.

Large-scale piracy in North American waters was for the most part eradicated by the increased naval activity and vigilance of authorities not long after 1720, but from time to time isolated acts of piracy occurred right into the nineteenth century. But it was in the full flower of the heady days of the so-called Golden Age of Piracy, in which the Lows and Cobhams and others of their ilk flourished, that Bartholomew Roberts would come north to the most formative experience of his brief career. It would be the experience that transformed him in one daring and brilliantly — if ruthlessly — executed attack from a minor open-ocean bandit to a heavily armed commander of a flotilla of ships, the flagship of which carried sufficient guns and men to challenge virtually any armed merchantman, and even certain categories of warship. This was "fleet piracy" of a scale unseen in those waters since Easton and Mainwaring. And when he finally swept south out of the north, Roberts would continue to build his power until virtually all of West Indian trade was at his mercy.[2]

It is intriguing to note that forty years later, another British seaman whose career had been undistinguished to that point was transformed by events in Canadian waters and his own talents into a notable — and noted — figure: James Cook, a taciturn Yorkshireman who arrived in North American waters in 1758 as sailing master of a British warship. He became an innovative coastal surveyor almost by chance during the siege of Louisbourg, and so distinguished himself by his service on the St. Lawrence and a later charting of the same Newfoundland coast where Roberts made his fateful raid that he was selected in 1768 to command the first of three epic voyages into the Pacific. Both men were reserved, self-controlled leaders, but utterly different as to motivation and principles. Yet it is interesting to note that for both men, who made such an impact on the world's maritime history, it would be the waters of what would become Canada that shaped them at a key moment.

That Roberts and other lawless men would be drawn to northern waters is readily explicable, as we have seen, but Dan Conlin expresses this clearly:

> Atlantic Canada was mostly populated by still-powerful native peoples. The few tiny colonies in Nova Scotia and Newfoundland were dwarfed by a massive seasonal fishery. Tens of thousands of English, French, Spanish, Basque and Portuguese fishermen arrived every spring to harvest the seemingly endless fishing wealth of the banks, the shallow and productive waters between Nova Scotia and Newfoundland. Year-round settlement was discouraged and government was close to non-existent — a perfect recipe for piracy.[3]

There is another part of the story of piracy in Canada that has been rarely written about, and that is how Mi'kmaq people became seamen of great skill, carrying out what amounted to piratical seizures of ships and boats, in their seagoing heyday between 1630 and the end of the Seven Years War. It is a little-known story that Conlin summarizes:

The Mi'kmaq themselves repeatedly claimed that their seizures of vessels were statements of territorial control.... Ships were seized to achieve immediate goals, such as ... reprisals, forcing prisoner exchanges or stopping unwelcome traders — especially of alcohol. But the seizing of ships also had a broader goal of controlling Mi'kmaq territory. Mi'kmaq sea raids, combined with their land attacks, confined English settlements in Atlantic Canada to a handful of locations.... The Mi'kmaq would sustain their attacks at sea until 1760, when a lasting peace was finally negotiated with the British.[4]

It was against the panorama of this complex and poorly understood saga of piracy in Canadian waters that the newly minted pirate Bartholomew Roberts, smarting from setbacks and humiliation, would sail into the north, there to be transformed into the most successful — if the word is apt — pirate of his age. And when he left those cold northern waters to steer southward, his black ensigns flying from his ships, he would embark on the climactic last year or two of a remarkable career that some would argue qualified him for the title king of the Atlantic pirates.

5

The Blade Unsheathed

It is one of the ironies of the Roberts story that the man he encountered far from home, off the coast of West Africa, the one who introduced him to the world of piracy, was, in fact, a fellow Welshman who came from a port barely a half-day's walk from Roberts's home village.

Howell Davis was a merchant seaman from Milford Haven, Wales, who had begun a career at sea much as Roberts had, in merchant shipping or in a Royal Navy ship. As Marcus Rediker observes, "By all accounts, by 1713 the Atlantic economy had reached a new stage of maturity, stability, and profitability. The growing riches of the few depended on the growing misery of the many."[1] Misery it might have been for common seamen, but the end of the war against Louis XIV had prompted a resumption of international trade — and a simultaneous surge in piracy on that shipping.

Davis appears to have begun his career in lawful service as a seaman, but also to have suffered, as many men did, at the hands of abusive masters of the ships he sailed in, so much so that by 1718 he was poised to enter the ranks of pirates in the West Indies. He had fetched up at New Providence in the Bahamas, a notorious pirate lair, and one to which a very competent ex-freebooter named Woodes Rogers was sent by the Crown to employ either the promise of royal pardon or the force of gunpowder to bring an end to the piracy bedevilling the Caribbean. Rogers arrived at New Providence in 1718, as well, and soon established royal authority with such vigour that there was a wholesale departure of pirate crews from the Bahamas across the Atlantic to the alluringly lawless West African coast and the potential prizes of slave ships operating there.

Davis had had previous first-hand experience with pirates: in that fateful year of 1718, he was serving as the first mate of a slaver, the *Cadogan*, which was taken by the pirate Edward England while off the Sierra Leone coast. Davis so impressed England with either his own agreeable manner or the support of the *Cadogan's* crew — pirates, as we have seen, often dealt savagely with the officers of captured ships whose crews complained of cruelty and mistreatment — that England turned the ship, crew, and cargo of slaves over to Davis, to do with as he wished. Davis stayed within the law and sailed to Barbados, where, regardless of his good intentions, he was thrown in jail for three months until cleared of piracy charges.

Perhaps a touch embittered, Davis took passage to New Providence, where he joined the crew of a provisioning sloop, the *Buck*. It was chartered into the King's service by Woodes Rogers; New Providence was short of supplies and the *Buck* was to sail to the American mainland for staples. Most of the crew were ex-pirates who had accepted the King's pardon, but their new loyalty did not last long. Within hours of sailing, they had mutinied, and due to his superior "artistry" as a seaman — and perhaps his appealing character — Davis found himself elected captain.

Now commanding sixty pirates and a sloop of six guns, but which could be armed with more, Davis made a few captures off the great island of Hispaniola. He realized that Woodes Rogers would soon be in grim pursuit of the *Buck* and those who had stolen her, so, rather than risking almost certain capture at Rogers's hands, Davis made the bold decision to make a transatlantic voyage to the West African coast, where other pirates had fled. As historian Angus Konstam explains:

> This was not a strange decision. The "bight" of West Africa was the area where most early eighteenth-century slave ships picked up their human cargo, either through established trading posts — many of them operated

by the Royal Africa Company or by the Portuguese — or else by dealing directly with the African rulers in towns such as Whydah (or Ouidah) and Calabar. Davis considered the coast a rich hunting ground, although his reasoning might also have been that he knew those waters better than the Caribbean. First the pirates visited the Cape Verde Islands, where Davis decided to put in to the small Portuguese island of Sao Nicolau. He spent a month there, having convinced the locals he was an English privateer. In February 1719 he broke his cover by raiding the roadstead of Porto Ingles, on the nearby island of Maio (Isle of May). The pirates helped themselves to whatever they could find from the small vessels in the harbour and then captured a much larger twenty-six-gun vessel called the *Loyal Merchant*, which chose the wrong time to enter the port. Davis renamed her *Royal James* ... and abandoned the *Buck*.... By February 23 the pirates were off the West African coast, having made landfall at ... the mouth of the Gambia River.[2]

That Davis made such a voyage successfully with a presumably turbulent crew speaks not only of his navigational skill and seamanship, but again of his evidently agreeable personality. The sailor William Snelgrave, who had been held prisoner by Davis for a time while off Sierra Leone, had come to respect him "because he kept his ship's company in good order [and was] a most generous humane person."[3]

Clearly Davis was a man of parts, if perhaps not entirely the "romantic Welshman filled with Arthurian chivalry [who] had sworn that he would never shame or hurt a gallant opponent," as claimed by another Roberts biographer, Aubrey Burl.[4]

If the *Royal James* was now to be pursuing either slaves or other valuable goods from the slaving fleet, it is likely that Davis and his men were as much concerned with simply helping themselves to the prosaic necessities of life as were most pirates. Pirate historian David Cordingly recounts:

> When the snow [ship] *Restoration* was attacked in August 1717, the pirates took all the goods and provisions on board as well as "sails, pump-bolts, log-lines, needles, twine, kettle, frying pan." The sloop *Content*, which was taken near Barbados in October 1723, was looted of "fourteen boxes of candles, and two boxes of soap, … flying-jib-halliards, main halliards, anchor and cable and several carpenters tools."[5]

Davis, who by this point had developed a piratical style based as much on guile and cunning as violence, now had to secure off Africa the necessities of life available only ashore, as well as the prospect of gainful loot. At the mouth of the Gambia River there was a small fortified trading station run by the Royal Africa Company, known as Gambia Castle, with a small surrounding village. Arriving with the ship flying the English merchant flag, Davis soon found that the post's fortifications were not complete and that the governor lived aboard an RAC vessel, the *Royal Ann*, anchored off the village. Until darkness fell, Davis maintained the fiction of being a merchantman, then went off quietly in the *Royal James*'s boats and took the *Royal Ann* — and presumably the governor — in a short, savage fight. That done, Davis's crew stormed ashore and quickly captured the unfinished fort and the village.

Davis's crew gave themselves over to a riot of looting, drinking, and chasing what women were available, pausing only to destroy what they could of the fort before welcoming the arrival of a fourteen-gun brig flying pirate colours that carried a French crew under the command of Olivier Levasseur. That crew gleefully flung themselves into the partying. The loot from the captured post was less than expected, but it took a further week of exhaustive debauchery before the crews of both vessels could be coaxed to stagger back aboard. The two vessels then sailed for Sierra Leone, where the pickings might be better. They met there another colleague in the "Sweet Trade."[6]

Pirates frequently allied in on-again, off-again relationships. As Marcus Rediker relates,

Pirates showed a recurrent willingness to join forces at sea and in port. In April 1719, when Howell Davis and crew sailed into the Sierra Leone River, the pirates captained by Thomas Cocklyn were wary until they saw on the approaching ship "her Black Flag"; then "immediately they were easy in their minds, and a little time after," the crews "saluted one another with their Cannon." Other crews exchanged similar greetings [and] frequently invoked an unwritten code of hospitality to forge spontaneous alliances.[7]

Both Cocklyn and the French captain had been part of the New Providence scene before Woodes Rogers arrived to spoil the fun, so the Sierra Leone meeting was a reunion of sorts. Over the clink and tumult of the celebrations — no excuse for a party carried to excess seemed ever to miss pirate attention — the three captains agreed that the affable Davis would command the flotilla. The decision was also made to try their luck on another fortified post a short distance away at the mouth of the Sierra Leone, which had the added attraction of six slavers or merchantmen seen at anchor under the fort's guns.

Guns or not, the fort soon fell to the furious pirate assault — the RAC would later claim that the garrison surrendered only when all gunpowder had been expended. The ships and fort were then thoroughly looted, leading again to weeks of paralytic drinking and debauchery, which, not unexpectedly, eventually ended the amicable temporary alliance of the three pirate crews.[8]

Captain Charles Johnson — possibly a pseudonym for Daniel Defoe — author of *A General History of the Pyrates*, recorded the falling-out:

> Having called a Counsel of War, they agreed to sail down the Coast together, and for the greater Grandeur, appointed a Commadore, which was *Davis*; but they had not kept Company long, when drinking together on board of *Davis*, they had like to have fallen together by

the Ears, the strong Liquor stirring up a Spirit of Discord among them, and they quarelled, but *Davis* put an End to it, by this short Speech: — *Heark ye, you* Cocklyn *and* La Bouse, *I find by strengthening you, I have put a Rod into your Hands to whip my self, but I'm still able to deal with you both; but since we met in Love, let us part in Love, for I find, that three of a Trade can never agree.* — Upon which the other two went on Board their respective Ships, and immediately parted, each steering a different Course.[9]

Davis carried on to the southeast, around the African coast, successfully taking and looting two British ships as he went before running into a Dutch vessel, the *Marquis del Campo*, of formidable strength, off Cape Three Points. The Dutch refused to surrender to Davis and forced a bloody, thirty-hour gun battle that Davis eventually won. The new prize was such a fine vessel of thirty guns that Davis shifted his flag into it, named it the *Royal Rover*, and turned the *Royal James* over to the command of a powerfully brutal and unpredictable member of his crew, Walter Kennedy. Kennedy had some gifts of coarse leadership, but no navigational skills. Later, he would be the cause of much trouble for Bartholomew Roberts.[10]

With *Royal James* following, Davis then shaped his course eastward along the Guinea coast, his goal the slaving port of Fort Charles at Anamaboe, where ships anchored off the coast to receive their wretched cargos of slaves. It was not a place remembered with affection, and its climate was so lethal to RAC employees that the posts of each were said to be listed not only by the incumbent governor's name, but that of his replacement at sea on the way to succeed him after his certain early death and of the man chosen to replace the replacement.

The Fanti fishing village and English trading station of Anamaboe on the Guinea Coast of Africa was the sort of place white men ventured to visit only out of greed. There could be no other reason. The furnace days under a blinding equatorial sun, the humid, windless nights, the poor food, resentful natives, and myriad tropical diseases made it an earthly hell for Europeans. Yet in 1719, Anamaboe was one of the richest and most important of the chain of permanent European posts along the West African littoral. The slave trade was then entering its most prosperous period, and Anamaboe, at the seaward end of an easy route from the interior, was among the busiest of the slaving entrepôts dotting the African bulge from the Senegal River to Whydah.[11]

Davis had avoided entering the three-mile extreme gun range of a more powerful RAC post, that of Cape Coast Castle, before arriving at Anamaboe, which lay a little over four leagues — about thirteen miles — east of it. On June 5, 1719, Davis found three ships lying at anchor off its harbourless beaches out beyond the surf line: the *Morrice*, the *Royal Hind*, and the *Princess* galley of London — a vessel able to be rowed with large sweeps if necessary. The *Princess* was loading her cargo while the other vessels had not yet completed their deals ashore, "trading for Negroes, Gold, and Teeth."[12]

As they approached the anchored vessels, Davis and Kennedy's ships looked menacing and dark, with their decks packed with armed men. The slavers dropped their ensigns and surrendered without a fight. Ashore, Fort Charles's guns fired a few token rounds at the pirates, but when Davis had *Royal Rover* fire a single full broadside in reply — his ship now armed with thirty-two long guns and twenty-seven swivels — the fort gave up any pretence of resistance. The exulting pirates, still smarting from the brutal battle with the *Marquis del Campo*, ran alongside the surrendered ships. An important event then took place, as Burl relates:

> The *Royal Rover* came alongside the *Princess* of London and nervously Stephenson, her second mate, asked what it was the pirate wanted him to do. His captain, Plumb, and the first mate were absent. Davis told him and his men to come aboard. The mate was followed by a chirpy

little fellow, John Eastwell, a carpenter, and six others: James Bradshaw, William Gittius, a gunner, John Jessup, John Owen and Thomas Rogers. The sixth and last man was the third mate…. He was tall, older than most, in his late thirties, broad-shouldered, dark-haired, with a swarthy, stern face brown from years at sea.

His name was Bartholomew Roberts.[13]

Longboats were lowered from the *Royal Rover* and the *Royal James*, and the pirates rowed in through the dangerous surf to burst into the fort ashore, brush aside the terrified garrison, and avail themselves of the provisions, ships' stores, liquor supplies, trade goods, and — dramatically — bags of coin and gold dust.

Out on the ships, Davis had lost nine men in the battle with the stubborn Dutch, and a total of thirty-five men were added to the two crews, with some volunteering, and some, like Roberts, forced. As historian Richard Sanders observes:

> With the capture of Roberts and the other thirty-four men on 6 June Davis was stronger than ever. As his men joyously plundered the liquor stores of the three ships that afternoon he was already considering trading up again. He set the Dutch crew of the *Marquis del Campo* free, but he kept their ship [now the *Royal Rover*] … handing them the *Morrice* to return home. Then, as the sun set, he weighed anchor and headed east … [with] his growing flotilla of prizes.[14]

Roberts has been identified in several accounts as a carpenter — a valuable trade to be in during the era of wooden sailing ships — but in addition soon demonstrated a knowledge of navigation and other arts of the mariner that indicated to Davis and others that he was an individual of considerable experience beyond that of a simple seaman. That experience had been gained either in the slave trade alone, or, as suggested, in combination with time in warships or privateers. As Charles Johnson relates when later describing Roberts's end, it did not take long for his initial resistance at joining the pirates to fade, first into acquiescence, and then into full and even enthusiastic acceptance:

> He could not plead Want of Employment, nor Incapacity of getting his Bread in an honest way, to favour so vile a change, nor was he so much a Coward as to pretend it; but frankly own'd, it was to get rid of the disagreeable Superiority of some Masters he was acquainted with, and the Love of Novelty and Change, Maritime Peregrinations had accustom'd him to. *In an honest Service,* says he, *there is thin Commons, low Wages, and hard Labour; in this, Plenty and Satiety, Pleasure and Ease, Liberty and Power; and who would not balance Creditor on this Side, when all the Hazard that is run for it, at worst, is only a sour Look or two at choaking. No, A merry Life and a short one, shall be my Motto.* Thus he preach'd himself into an Approbation of what he first abhorr'd; and being daily regal'd with Musick, Drinking, and the Gaiety and Diversions of his Companions, these deprav'd Propensities were quickly edg'd and strengthened, to the extinguishing of Fear and Conscience. Yet among all the vile and ignominious Acts he had perpetrated, he is said to have had an Aversion towards forcing Men into that Service, and had procured some their Discharge, notwithstanding so many made it their Plea.[15]

The capture that had brought Roberts into the pirate fold was, like so many similar experiences, a relatively bloodless one. In contrast to the earlier semi-savage buccaneers of coastal Hispaniola, who arguably were the progenitors of the European pirate phenomenon, the open-ocean pirates gave much visual evidence of readiness for bloody conflict, but in reality were not disposed toward it at all, except for the murderous or psychopathic within their ranks. Stanley Richards observes succinctly the reasons for this:

The taking of these three vessels without bloodshed was very typical of the operations of pirates in those days. Pirates differed in this respect from buccaneers in that they were not a bloodthirsty fraternity spoiling for a fight. It was their ambition to acquire plunder and live to enjoy the pleasures that it brought them. A battle might deprive them of that life of ease. Hence on the chance occasions when they had to go into action against another ship it was looked upon by them as almost a repulsive necessity. They were after booty, not blood.

Their whole strategy was shaped to obtain wealth without having to fight for it. Thus they sought to frighten their victims into surrender with such aids as the brandishing of cutlasses, the displaying of black flags emblazoned with a skeletal apparition representing death, the banging and blowing of instruments. But above all was their threat to kill if resistance were offered to them, and they let the world know this. When they were resisted, pirates usually killed their victims without mercy. The consequence was that it was seldom they had to fight, and a merchantman when she beheld the death's head of the pirate flag hauled down her own colours and asked for good quarter, thereby signalling her complete surrender providing that all lives were to be spared. Generally speaking, the captives were not afterwards ill-treated.[16]

This preference for bloodless captures goes against the modern perception of mindless, oath-filled violence visited against all who crossed pirates' wakes — although certainly the Cobhams off Newfoundland demonstrated that stereotype — but it appears in several interpretations to derive from the origins of many pirates, who were largely merchant seamen who had suffered at the hands of greedy, callous, or brutal shipmasters. This led them to be prepared to be forbearing and almost solicitous of captured crews out of a sense of shared experience. The pirates were all too aware that the structure of eighteenth-century society and the mechanisms of trade were not intended to favour them, or even to use them as anything beyond a pool of expendable labour in the pursuit of wealth and profit for a tiny social minority. The greater revolutionary movements had yet to surface in European society, and the pyramidic hierarchy of privilege and social limitation in a vastly unfair system was as yet unchallenged except by the stirrings in the minds of a few, such as the so-called Levellers of the previous century.

In their own way, the despair and fatalism of the pirates led them to introduce among themselves a kind of crude equality, but also a social consciousness that would have made a Marxist's eyes gleam: it was not, however, a thought that crossed a pirate's mind as he grasped, however fleetingly, at the riches and material goods he could otherwise never have had, and waited in an alcoholic haze of plunder, debauchery, and self-gratification for the inevitable hammer of the law to fall. They were dead men, and they knew it, but for some at least the "Sweet Trade" provided a glimpse of egalitarianism and humanity they might otherwise never have known.

In a violent, brutal age there lay in their crude shipboard "commonwealths" arguably the glimmers of what more articulate men would express in the revolutionary movements of later years, beginning in the English-speaking world out of which they sprang. There would be exceptions, of course: some pirate vessels were run as rigidly as any warship. But by and large the idea of a small democracy at sea was not far off the mark for most.

Upon leaving Anamaboe, Davis led his flotilla eastward along the African coast, his mind turning to the need for his ship — or ships — to be careened in order for weed-fouled bottoms to be scraped and cleaned and the crews "refreshed." One need that pirates always had was for "a shift of clothes," which was a prize awarded often for pirate crews after a capture, suggesting that common clothing deteriorated rapidly at sea, and that the clothing on captives or in goods taken in ships was not for each man to seize at will, but was handed out as a reward. The image of bandana-wearing, semi-ragged ruffians may not have been far from the true picture of a pirate crew long between captures, and one pirate is known to have taken a ship merely to secure a supply of hats. After his successful venture at Anamaboe, Davis presumably had a better-dressed crew.

Soon after the departure from Anamaboe, the flotilla came upon a Dutch vessel that wisely surrendered after Davis's first warning gun. The ship proved to be carrying the governor of the Dutch trading post of Accra on the Slave Coast, and, more importantly, some fifteen thousand pounds' worth of gold in coin and a quantity of trade goods. This clearly called for a celebratory event, and Davis behaved true to his generous form, freeing all the prisoners except those who declared their willingness to stay with him, and releasing the remaining prizes, as well, leaving only the *Royal Rover* and the *Royal James*. But as the ships worked into the Gulf of Guinea and approached the mouth of what was then known to the Portuguese as the Rio Camarones, the crew of the *Royal James* could not keep up with the pumps against a hull leak — likely due to planking riven by the teredo worm, or naval shipworm — and the decision was made to abandon the ship. Kennedy's crew and anything useful was transferred to the *Royal Rover*, and the *Royal James* was set adrift and set afire. A port was now a vital necessity.

There is a chain of islands lying fifty to two hundred miles off the West African coast, which were claimed in the 1500s by the Portuguese as they developed their trade routes around Africa into the Indian Ocean: Fernando Po; Principe (or Prince's Island, now Principe); Sao Thome (São Tomé); and Annaboe (Annobón), not to be confused with the coastal post of similar name. Prince's Island lies just above the equator, and it was toward this well-settled island that Davis turned *Royal Rover*'s jib-boom. Making landfall of the principal harbour in little more than a day, Davis replied to an inquiry sent out by a guard boat that *Royal Rover* was an English warship pursuing pirates. The island's governor approved their arrival and provided a pilot to help *Royal Rover* work into the harbour, where Davis correctly provided a gun salute that was answered by the protecting fort. It is not difficult to imagine Davis and his mates dressed more or less as officers and succeeding with the masquerade. In 1718, officers were distinguished more by "a rattan and a string of oaths" than the more gentlemanly traits encouraged later, and a naval uniform did not exist for the Royal Navy until 1748.

For the crew of *Royal Rover*, Prince's Island offered not only the prospect of a safe careening and replenishment port, but other attractions as well, which Stanley Richards lists:

> The harbour had openings into smaller, sandy coves convenient for camping ashore, watering and careening. At that time the whole approach to the town, which was at the head of the bay and consisted of two or three streets of wooden-built houses, was protected by a fort having a battery of 12 guns. The isle did not, however, hold for the pirates the protection afforded by Hispaniola nor the shelter and convenience of the spider's web of Sierre Leone.
>
> The isle appeared to be an earthly paradise, and an ideal spot for sailors stricken with scurvy since it had an abundance of trees, fruits, vegetables and animals. But it was infested with malaria and, if that were not enough, venereal disease was rampant in this *Arcadia* for, although temperate and abstemious in their other habits, the islanders were unbounded in their lusts.[17]

Prince's Island had indeed a quality that was not unlike what Tahiti would offer or other idyllic islands, remote as they were from the problems of the mainland. Davis now had to undertake the arduous but necessary task of careening *Royal Rover*. Having spent a long time in tropic waters, the bottom of the hull was heavily fouled with weed, barnacles, and other growths, and the planking had been weakened by the ravages of the teredo worm.

Davis brought the ship round to a sandy cove that had been found by the ship's longboat, where a gently sloping shore and beach with shelter under the palms inshore made for a desirable "careenage." The ship was worked in as far as possible and then lightened in several days' worth of work. Guns, spars, anchors, gear, and the contents of the hold were got ashore, and the crew set up an encampment under the trees, using the ship's sails as tents. The upper masts were struck down, and the ship was then manoeuvred so that it lay broadside to the shore. A series of tackles (pronounced "taykles") were then fixed to the tops of the remaining lower masts and led ashore to sturdy roots or trees. With all hands tailing on to the "falls" (the lines of the tackles to be pulled upon), the ship was hauled over onto its side, revealing the fouled bottom. With scraping irons and even flaming torches to burn off stubborn weed growth, the men worked under the blazing sun to scrape and clean the planking. Planks needing repair were replaced by the carpenters, and then the planking was caulked, likely with "oakum" spun out from old rope. The final act was to coat the visible planks with a mixture of sulphur and tallow, to hopefully slow new growth. Then the ship had to be eased upright, turned to present its uncleaned side, and hauled down once more. It was slow, tedious work, but Davis and his men knew that a decent sailing speed was key to their survival and to successful captures. But, as Richards observes, "the task ashore went on in a leisurely manner, and any boredom was soon forgotten as the evenings were given over to wine and women."[18]

A brief interlude almost led to Davis's true identity being revealed to the Portuguese, however. A French ship put into the harbour to purchase supplies, and Davis and his crew immediately pounced on it, reporting to the astonished Portuguese, as Johnson relates, that "[the French ship] had been trading with the Pyrates, and that he found several Pyrates Goods on Board, which he seized for the King's Use: This story passed so well upon the Governor, that he commended *Davis's* Diligence."

If the Portuguese governor had had any suspicions about Davis's true identity before this point, he certainly had grounds for them now. But no sign came.[19]

Davis was no fool, and likely thought that neither was the governor. Sensing that he was figuratively in shallow waters, Davis now turned to his next objective:

> Having cleaned his Ship, and put all Things in Order, his Thoughts now were turned upon the main Business, *viz.* the Plunder of the Island, and not knowing where the Treasure lay, a Stratagem came into his Head, to get it (as he thought) with little Trouble, he consulted his Men upon it, and they liked the Design: His Scheme was, to

make a Present to the Governor, of a Dozen Negroes, by Way of Return for the Civilities received from him, and afterwards to invite him, with the chief Men, and some of the Friers, on Board his Ship, to an Entertainment; the Minute they came on Board, they were to be secured in Irons, and there kept till they should pay a Ransom of 40000 *l.* Sterling.[20]

Things were starting to unravel for Davis: an attempt by him and some of his men to get ashore and find more willing women in the town had come to naught, and a man had run to the governor with news of the unseemly effort when the respectable women had fled to the woods. This same man may also have warned the governor of Davis's plot to hold him hostage for ransom; the story is unclear. But a day before Davis planned to sail, he undertook to put the plan in motion by going to the governor's house in all seeming innocence. The jig may already have been up: as Richards relates, "it seems, however, that the islanders soon discovered that Davis and his followers were pirates, and not officers and men of the Royal Navy ... but the Governor winked at their profession because of the profits he and others made."[21]

Having received the governor's earlier acceptance to Davis's invitation to go aboard *Royal Rover* for hospitality, Davis soon found that he had been outwitted:

The next day *Davis* went on Shore himself, as if it were out of greater Respect to bring the Governor on Board: He was received with the usual Civility, and he, and other principal Pyrates, who, by the Way, had assumed the Title of Lords, and as such took upon them to advise or councel their Captain upon any important Occasion; and likewise held certain Priviledges, which the common Pyrates were debarr'd from, as walking the Quarter-Deck, using the great Cabin, going ashore at Pleasure, and treating with foreign Powers, that is, with the Captains of Ships they made Prize of; I say, *Davis* and some of the

Lords were desired to walk up to the Governor's House, to take some Refreshment before they went on Board; they accepted it without the least Suspicion, but never returned again; for an Ambuscade was laid, a Signal being given, a whole Volley was fired upon them; they every Man dropp'd, except one, this one fled back, and escaped into the Boat, and got on Board the Ship: *Davis* was shot through the Bowels, yet he rise again, and made a weak Effort to get away, but his Strength soon forsook him, and he dropp'd down dead; just as he fell, he perceived he was followed, and drawing out his Pistols, fired them at his Pursuers; Thus like a game Cock, giving a dying Blow, that he might not fall unrevenged.[22]

According to other accounts, the governor had placed armed men outside the governor's residence, and they opened fire at a signal from one of the governor's staff. Davis's end was a dramatic one, and other accounts add more detail:

Captain Davis, though he had four shots in various parts of his body, continued to retreat in an orderly fashion toward the boat, but he was closely pursued and a fifth shot brought him down. As he dropped he levelled his pistols and fired at his pursuers, killing two of them.... His assailants ... cut his throat so that they might be sure that he would not harm them further.[23]

The survivor panted back to the boat with the Portuguese in hot pursuit, and, in a lather of rowing the boat, made it back to the ship with the news of the killing of Davis and the others. The pirates were enraged and in a mood for bloody revenge, but they were leaderless. It would be necessary to elect a captain who, if only first among equals, would have the ability to lead them in any attack.

Davis had kept order in the crew through personal example and a good deal of charm, but the angry, frustrated assembly on the deck of the *Royal Rover* was anything but orderly. As Johnson's account reveals, the crew had become divided between the "Lords," who were the long-service and more experienced men, and the "Commons," who were not. There was tension in this division and there were also restless, brutal men who were good in a fight but ill-suited to accepting authority of any kind. One such was the Irishman Walter Kennedy, described by Johnson as "a bold daring Fellow, but very wicked and profligate." He would later prove to be a dangerous and almost fatal problem for Bartholomew Roberts.[24]

The debate went on, and attention was soon drawn to the tall, quiet figure of Bartholomew Roberts, who had been in the ship for barely six weeks and had initially resisted invitations to join the crew. Somehow in those weeks, Roberts's skill at the seaman's arts — navigation, seamanship, gunnery, weapons, ship management — had come to the fore; he had been warmly tutored and encouraged by Davis, who spoke Welsh with him for secrecy, and there must have been some unique quality in his character that struck a spark in the hard-edged men of the *Royal Rover*. A member of the "Lords," who may have been Dennis McCarty, stepped forward and nominated Roberts for the captaincy:

> *We are the original of this Claim* (says he) *and should a Captain be so sawcy as to exceed Prescription at any time, why down with Him! It will be a Caution after he is dead to his Successors, of what fatal Consequence any sort of assuming may be. However, it is my Advice, that, while we are sober, we pitch upon a Man of Courage, and skill'd in Navigation, one, who by his Counsel and Bravery seems best able to defend this Commonwealth, and ward us from the Dangers and Tempests of an instable Element, and the fatal Consequences of Anarchy; and such a one I take* Roberts *to be. A Fellow! I think, in all Respects, worthy [of] your Esteem and Favour.*[25]

There was hearty applause for this nomination from most of the crew — one man, Sympson, who had wanted the role, grumbled but finally admitted, "*he did not care who they chose Captain, so* [long as] *it was not a Papist, for against them he had conceiv'd an irreconcileable Hatred.*"

The position was offered to Roberts, and "he accepted of the Honour, saying, *That since he had dipp'd his hands in muddy Water, and must be a Pyrate, it was better being a Commander than a common Man.*"[26]

And so Captain Roberts he now was.

It was not long before Roberts demonstrated that he would be a man of action. To the pirates' delight, he proposed an immediate assault ashore to avenge Davis and the other casualties. Walter Kennedy figured largely in the plan, and whether Roberts alone determined on the shore attack plan or did it in concert with Kennedy, the scheme was soon set.

Kennedy would command an armed party to land ashore on the steeply sloping land immediately before the harbour fort, while Roberts would work *Royal Rover* in through sail-handling or warping on anchor lines until the ship's broadside bore on the fort. As Kennedy's men approached the shore in their longboat, Roberts opened fire on the fort, elevating guns to bear on the ramparts and gun embrasures. With the ship's guns thundering behind them, Kennedy and his men charged up the steep slope, looking for a way into the fortification. No answering fire withered the pirates as they struggled up the slope; when Roberts's guns opened fire, the Portuguese garrison and gun crews, appalled at the sudden rain of well-aimed shot, had bolted from the fort. Kennedy and his men burst in to find themselves in full possession of the place without a struggle. As the smoke of the bombardment drifted away in low clouds from the waiting *Royal Rover*, Kennedy and his men set about throwing the fort's guns out through the embrasures to tumble down the slope to the sea, then set the wooden buildings within the walls on fire.

With flames leaping up over the ramparts behind them, Kennedy's men rollicked back down to their boat and rowed out to the waiting *Royal Rover*, likely to a few gratified cheers.

Once aboard, however, the pirates still thirsted for more revenge, and they pressed Roberts to lead them in a land attack on the town itself. Roberts saw that they might have rushed along the shore in impetuous haste, their anger leaving them open to a fatal counterattack by the

Portuguese. As Johnson relates, Roberts's tactical wisdom still gave the pirates some satisfying destruction:

> [M]ost of the Company were for burning the Town, which *Roberts* said he would yield to, if any Means could be proposed of doing it without their own Destruction, for the Town had a securer Scituation than the Fort, a thick Wood coming almost close to it, affording Cover to the Defendants, who under such an Advantage, he told them, it was to be fear'd, would fire and stand better to their Arms; besides, that bare Houses would be but a slender Reward for their Trouble and Loss. This prudent Advice prevailed; however, they mounted the *French* ship, they seiz'd at this Place, with 12 guns, and light'ned her, in order to come up to the Town, the Water being shoal, and battered down several Houses; after which they all returned on Board, gave back the *French* ship to those that had most Right to her, and sailed out of the Harbour by the light of two *Portuguese* Ships, which they were pleased to set on Fire there.[27]

As the *Royal Rover* ghosted out of the harbour, lit by the flames towering up from the burning ships, Roberts stood on its quarterdeck with the knowledge that he had demonstrated both the action and audacity that the pirates demanded of their leaders, but also a prudent caution and canny tactical sense.

To the men tightening down the rig for sea and glancing up at the tall figure on the quarterdeck, it must have seemed that they had made the right choice for captain. They could not have known how extraordinarily true that would prove to be in the three tumultuous years that lay ahead of them. They, and Roberts, were embarked on a voyage that would ultimately bring them to the waters of what would become Canada, where he would be transformed from an unremarkable pirate of little note into the most fearsome and successful pirate of the age.

6

Armed to the Teeth

Now that Roberts commanded the thirty-two-gun *Royal Rover*, with its hard-bitten crew watchful of his suitability to lead them, it likely occurred to Roberts that he would have to continue to prove his right to command, notwithstanding the effective attack on Prince's Island. He would have to prove that he could take ships, and secure what his crew both needed and wanted; he would have to demonstrate that he indeed had the "artistry" of navigation, which the majority of pirates did not, and could set proper courses for their voyaging; and lastly, he would have to demonstrate that he possessed those key traits of a pirate commander: courage and cunning. It would not be long before the newly minted captain, a tad older than his crew at thirty-seven years of age, would be pressed to demonstrate all three.

Clearing the harbour of Prince's Island, Roberts turned the *Royal Rover*'s jib-boom south, on a long reach down the island chain. Within a few days, a strange sail was spotted, and proved to be a Dutch merchantman. Roberts showed little hesitation and pounced on it, but gave the first inklings of his character as a leader when, after the Dutch ship was relieved of anything the pirates needed, the ship was restored to the Dutch and they were sent on their way. It was Roberts's first prize taken at sea while in command, and the absence of brutality would become a mark of most — but by no means all — of his subsequent captures.

Two days after he released the Dutch ship, his southward track brought him to the waters off Cape Lopez, which projects out from the African coast. There he encountered the Royal Africa Company ship *Experiment*, which had a long history of service on that coast. The capture went smoothly — surrender immediately following the hoisting of black flags or the firing of a warning gun — and, remarkably, virtually all the *Experiment*'s crew volunteered to join the pirates. Along with the few who were reluctant to do so, they were taken aboard and their ship set on fire. It would not be the last RAC vessel to suffer at Roberts's hands.[1]

With the assault on Prince's Island and two effective captures at sea to his credit, Roberts was meeting his crew's expectations at least to that point. He now steered for the waters off São Tomé to see if prey could be found there. Finding none, he turned southwest and reached the last island in the chain, some 110 miles from São Tomé and known at the time as Annabona. Here, they anchored off the principal harbour, San Antonio, and were able to obtain fresh water and other provisions from the lush island. But it was clear they had to decide on their next course of action.

A crew vote was held, with the choices being the Brazilian coast or the distant archipelago of the East Indies. Brazil was the choice, and Roberts managed to succeed in his second major test by navigating *Royal Rover* in the tricky doldrums and the equatorial countercurrent to the Brazilian coast in the respectable time of twenty-eight days. Their landfall was, in fact, a cluster of twenty-one islands and small rocky islets of great beauty known as Fernando de Noronha, which lies just over two hundred miles off the mainland.

Here, they were able to replenish their water and food supplies at leisure, and improved their ship's performance by "boot topping," which meant scraping weed and barnacles off the hull along the waterline and covering as much of the scraped hull as possible with a mixture of sulphur and tallow. It was not a complete careening, but it did improve a weed-fouled vessel's performance. This done, Roberts prepared a plan of sailing along the Brazilian coast just out of sight of land, ready to pounce on any ships bound for or departing the Portuguese colony. This was navigation raised to a remarkable level.[2]

That Roberts had taken the *Royal Rover* across the South Atlantic with accuracy and without accident was more remarkable than it seemed, given the state of navigation in that era. As David Cordingly observes:

> Considering the primitive state of navigation and charts in the early part of the eighteenth century it is surprising that more pirate ships were not wrecked. Any competent ship's master could determine latitude by measuring the altitude of the sun at midday with a quadrant or back-staff and making some simple calculations, but until the introduction of lunar distance tables in the 1760s, and John Harrison's invention of the marine chronometer around the same time, there was no accurate method of finding longitude at sea. This meant that a mariner could find out to within five or ten miles where he was in a north-south direction, but could not be certain where he was in an east-west direction.[3]

In summary, navigation in the era of Roberts was notoriously a matter of "lead, latitude, and lookout," and the principal concern was always to see a landfall before running into it.

Roberts had shown his gang of desperados that he had the knack of taking ships, and could navigate; there remained only the need to prove that he had that unfazed courage the pirates respected above all qualities. An opportunity soon presented itself to show that he had it, to a full measure. The plan of sailing slowly just off the Brazilian coast proved fruitless; however, and after several weeks of scanning nothing but empty horizons, the *Royal Rover* demanded a vote on what to do next. The vote was to return to the West Indies and its easier pickings. Roberts agreed, and stood in to the Brazilian coast to determine their position before laying a course northward around the eastern bulge of Brazil. As it happened, they made landfall off Baya de Todos os Sanctos, or All Saints' Bay, and were astonished to see riding at anchor in the wide bay forty-two Portuguese merchant ships, heavily laden and seemingly well-armed, and a short distance away two towering seventy-gun major warships of the Portuguese navy, likely preparing to escort the fleet to Lisbon.

A prudent course of action might have been to retire to seaward to await the convoy's sailing, then trail it to pick off slower stragglers or wanderers, keeping always to windward of the escorts. Roberts, who was already claimed by some as a man "of good natural parts and personal bravery," had other ideas. From some small craft at the mouth of the bay he took aboard a few hapless locals and established somehow the perils of the bay. Then, Roberts astonished his men by putting the helm over

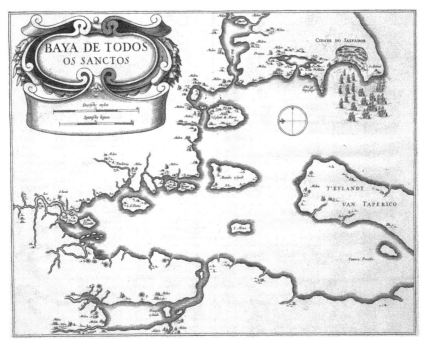

Crossing from West Africa early in his pirate career, Roberts cruised the Brazilian coast for weeks looking unsuccessfully for prey. In June of 1719 he entered this spacious bay, where he found forty-two heavily laden Portuguese ships anchored off the community of Salvador, waiting to sail for Portugal, with an escort of two warships. In an act of extreme daring, Roberts sailed into the midst of the fleet, captured a forty-gun ship, the Sagrada Familia *of Lisbon, then managed to escape without being opposed. The Portuguese ship would later be found to be carrying an immense treasure. This was the first of such captures by Roberts.*

and calmly steering directly into the middle of the huge, anchored formation. Richards relates what happened next:

> Ordering the bulk of his men below until he could weigh up the possibilities in his mind and resolve upon a course of action, he sailed in leisurely among the shipping. It then dawned on him that the answer to his problem was to make his intended victims disclose where their wealth lay; so he crept up to one of the deepest laden. Hailing her crew, he ordered them to send their commander aboard him, at the same time threatening to give them no quarter if any resistance or signal of distress were made. The Portuguese, take by surprise and cowed by the flourish of cutlasses of the crew who had suddenly reappeared on deck, submitted without a word and their captain went aboard. Roberts saluted him in a friendly manner, and told him that they were *gentlemen of fortune,* but that all he wanted from him was to be informed which was the richest ship in the fleet. If he directed them rightly, Roberts promised him that he should be restored to his command without harm, but otherwise he must expect instant death. The captain perforce quickly made his decision, and pointed to the *Sagrada Familia* (Holy Family), a vessel of forty cannon and 150 men, which alone was more than a match for the [*Royal*] *Rover*.[4]

Roberts — who clearly had some fluency in the Portuguese language, or a crewman who did — eyed the forty-gunner and calmed his apprehensive crew, saying that they were merely facing the Portuguese. Then he steered for the *Sagrada*. As he approached in a light wind, his men hid below the bulwarks except for sail handlers and those on the helm. Roberts affected an air of calm and ordered the captain of the merchantman to hail the *Sagrada*, asking that its captain cross to the *Royal Rover* for an important discussion. The *Sagrada*'s captain hailed back that he would be pleased to cross over directly. But the ruse, Roberts could see, was clearly not working, as frantic activity began on the forty-gunner's decks. It was time to act before all was lost. Below, *Royal Rover*'s gunners had been waiting at their guns, linstocks smouldering. Roberts barked out the command to fire, and the side of *Royal Rover* erupted with a thunderous broadside that smashed into the *Sagrada*'s hull. With clouds of smoke billowing between and around the two ships, Roberts ordered his men up from where they hid behind the bulwarks, and ordered the helm put hard over, steering *Royal Rover* to come close alongside the larger vessel. As it hit with a grinding crash, Roberts ordered grapnels flung over to bind the ships together. Then Walter Kennedy, at the head of a heavily armed knot of pirates, went over the side with a roar at Roberts's command and the pirates flung themselves against the Portuguese. There was a furious struggle, the clash of blade on blade, the blasts of muskets and pistols, and the shrieks of wounded men. But the pirates would not be denied. The fighting was vicious, but short, and soon Kennedy and his men had the deck, with many Portuguese killed or wounded, but only two of the pirates.

Stunned into action by this furious assault in the midst of the anchored convoy, crews of the merchantmen made desperate signals with guns and loosed topsails to get the attention of the Portuguese warships. Roberts could see, however, that the escorts were not responding with alacrity. He called across to Kennedy to secure the remaining Portuguese below and get the *Sagrada* underway quickly. Sails thumped down from the ship's yards as pirates scrambled aloft, the grapnels were cast off, the cable cut with axe blows, and *Sagrada* began to make way out of the anchorage, steering for the open sea, with *Royal Rover* following. As yet, no other merchantman had fired on the pirates. Roberts looked ahead. He was braced up hard to get to windward of the two anchored warships, which they would have to pass closely to get to sea. *Sagrada* was proving the less weatherly, and Kennedy was at its stern rail shouting back that he might not be able to weather the warships. Roberts could see otherwise, however, and he ordered Kennedy to press on. In slow majesty the two ships ghosted out past the two seventy-gun warships, succeeding in clearing them barely by a musket shot off their bows. Tensely expecting a destructive thunder of guns from the Portuguese,

Roberts and Kennedy were astonished that no resistance was offered as they glided past. Within minutes the two ships were standing out to sea, the pirates on both ships hoarsely jubilant in disbelief at their spectacular success. In the *Royal Rover*, the incredulous pirates now looked at the tall, calm figure of Roberts on the quarterdeck with new respect: he had passed the greatest test they could demand of him. As Richards observes, "never in the gamut of stories of the sea was there such an amazing feat of gallantry as that of the lone [*Royal*] *Rover*, when she challenged ... such a mighty fleet of heavily-armed antagonists."[5]

Once at sea and standing to the northward on course for the Caribbean, the crews had an opportunity to get below in the prize ship and see what their daring move had won. And a substantial haul it was: "A fabulous treasure of 40,000 moidores valued at more than 50,000 pounds sterling, beautiful jewels, chains, trinkets, sugar, tobacco and hides [and] a beautiful cross set with diamonds which had been designed for no less a figure that the king of Portugal."[6]

With swag of this quantity in hand, the pirates were anxious to find a welcoming haven where the booty could be shared out, provisions found, and enjoyment secured. They found such a haven at Devil's Island, then a backwater Spanish colony near the mouth of the Suriname River on the northeast coast of South America. As researcher Donald G. Shomette relates,

> Here the pirates secured their welcome from the governor and his subordinates by presenting them with the diamond-studded cross as a bribe. For weeks the sea rovers lingered at Devil's Island, pouring their booty into gambling, rum, women, and self-indulgences of every kind. Roberts, unlike his comrades, was a tea drinker, and while permitting his men to debauch themselves, kept a wary eye open for any opportunity that might present itself.[7]

That opportunity was not long in appearing. Roberts had his orgy-weary crews sail to the mainland coast at the Suriname's mouth, where a small sloop out of Rhode Island came in sight and was quickly captured. The captain of the Rhode Island vessel disarmed the pirates with his agreeable nature, saying they were welcome to both his little vessel and its cargo, but that another Rhode Island vessel, a brigantine laden with general provisions, had sailed with him and was due there in a few days at most. Roberts kept the sloop, its crew, and its captain as unwilling guests and had a doubled watch set aloft to see if the brigantine could be spotted before it reached port. Ever needful of basic provisions, the pirates saw to a degree a greater value in the prosaic but wholesome goods the brigantine presumably carried than the gold and silver coins that bought rum or a prostitute's body but none of the basic needs of life.

It was not long before a lookout reported the topsails of the brigantine visible on the northern horizon one afternoon. The approach of that vessel was the beginning of a traumatic series of events for Roberts that would set him on a course through betrayal and defeat to northern waters, regrouping and restoring there, and a return to the southern hunting grounds, transformed into the Atlantic's most effectively equipped pirate, and arguably its most successful of the era. The sighting ignited a plan in Roberts's mind for the brigantine's capture. He would take the Rhode Island sloop, sloops being usually weatherly and handy vessels, and forty men, and stand out to intercept and take the brigantine. As the winds lay at the time, he apparently calculated the capture could be done the same day. The *Sagrada* and the *Royal Rover* he would leave behind under the command of the volatile Walter Kennedy. Roberts sailed off with little preparation, and the result, as Charles Johnson relates here, was a near disaster:

> [F]or *Roberts*, thinking of nothing less than bringing in the Brigantine that Afternoon, never troubled his Head about the Sloop's Provision, nor inquired what there was on Board to subsist such a Number of Men; but out he sails after his expected Prize, which he not only lost further Sight of, but after eight Days contending with contrary Winds and Currents, found themselves thirty Leagues to Leeward. The Current still opposing

their Endeavours, and perceiving no Hopes of beating up to their Ship, they came to an Anchor, and inconsiderately sent away the Boat to give the rest of the Company Notice of their Condition, and to order the Ship to them; but too soon, even the next Day, their Wants made them sensible of their Infatuation, for their Water was all expended, and they had taken no thought how they should be supply'd, till either the Ship came, or the Boat returned, which was not likely to be under five or six Days. Here, like *Tantalus*, they almost famished in Sight of the fresh Streams and Lakes; being drove to such Extremity at last that they were forced to tare up the Floor of the Cabin, and patch up a sort of Tub or Tray with Rope Yarns, to paddle ashore, and fetch off immediate Supplies of Water to preserve Life.[8]

After several days the sloop's boat returned from the anchorage at the mouth of the Suriname River with the stunning news that the local population had said the great Portuguese prize and the *Royal Rover*, under the presumed command of Kennedy, had sailed several days previously, abandoning Roberts and the men in the sloop to whatever fate awaited them. It was a staggering act of treachery, and the bitter lesson was not lost on Roberts — that there would have to be a form of discipline and enforced loyalty in dealing with such men, if only to ensure survival. It would later appear that Kennedy, once clear of the South American coast, listened to entreaties of some of the men who wanted no more of piracy except to vanish ashore in America or England with their booty. He surprised the agreeable Rhode Island captain of Roberts's sloop with the gift of the ponderous *Sagrada*, the return of his crew and several other hands, and the unlooted remainder of the cargo. The thunderstruck Yankee sailed off in his new command with warm thanks to Kennedy. Kennedy, for his part, sailed off in the general direction of Barbados — neither he nor anyone aboard could navigate — and began an aimless wandering cruise of the Caribbean until, after the capture of a Virginian vessel off Jamaica, the internal tensions in the pirate crew under Kennedy's captaincy came to a head. The story is worth relating in Johnson's original text:

> Some Days after the taking of the *Virginia* Man ... in cruising in the Latitude of *Jamaica*, *Kennedy* took a Sloop bound thither from *Boston*, loaded with Bread and Flower; aboard of this Sloop went all the Hands who were for breaking the Gang, and left those behind that had a Mind to pursue further Adventures. Among the former were *Kennedy*, their Captain, of whose Honour they had such a dispicable Notion, that they were about to throw him over-board, when they found him in the Sloop, as fearing he might betray them all, at their return to *England*; he having in his Childhood been bred a Pick-pocket, and before he became a Pyrate, a House-breaker; both Professions that these Gentlemen have a very mean Opinion of. However, Captain *Kennedy*, by taking solemn Oaths of Fidelity to his Companions, was suffered to proceed with them.
>
> In this Company there was but one that pretended to any skill in Navigation, (for *Kennedy* could neither write nor read, he being preferred to the Command merely for his Courage, which indeed he had often signaliz'd, particularly in taking the *Portuguese* Ship,) and he proved to be a Pretender only; for shaping their Course to *Ireland*, where they agreed to land, they ran away to the North-West Coast of *Scotland*, and there were tost about by hard Storms of Wind for several Days, without knowing where they were, and in great Danger of perishing: At length they pushed the Vessel into a little Creek, and went all ashore, leaving the Sloop at an Anchor for the next Comers.[9]

The arrival of the pirates on the Scottish coast began a series of ill-considered adventures for them all, their loud and spendthrift ways bringing them rapidly to the attention of suspicious authorities. Before long they were apprehended and brought to justice. Kennedy himself managed to weasel clear of early entrapment and actually made it to Ireland for a time before ending up back in London, where he used what was left of his personal haul from the *Sagrada* to set himself up as a brothel keeper. From that unsavoury career he was unearthed by the testimony of one of his women to whom he had bragged about his piracies, and who had as a client a Mate of one of the ships Kennedy had attacked. By that man's identification Kennedy was arrested, and finally hanged at Execution Dock on the Thames waterfront on July 19, 1721. In a sense, all pirates were dead men from the beginning of their careers, but one wonders what the career of the violent, brutish Kennedy might have been had he not betrayed Roberts on the Suriname River's shore.

The treachery of Kennedy and those who went with him outline the tenuous nature of pirate-crew relationships and loyalties; tenuous perhaps because both merchant sailors and naval seamen were accustomed to an arbitrary imposition of discipline governed by the whim of a merchant captain or the regulations governing the navy. Some scholars have argued that in their seagoing republics, as we have inferred before, were examples of democratic arrangements in a supremely undemocratic age; others argue that whatever arrangements pirates made for their own governance they drew on traditions from ashore, such as craft guilds or agricultural sharing societies. Whatever the truth, the tension between the heady freedom of undisciplined pirate existence and the need for organization or rules to ensure simple survival created circumstances like Kennedy's betrayal that pirates had to resolve if they were to survive the rigours of seafaring and the risks of a criminal life. They were experimenting socially, and the results were intriguing, as Marcus Rediker observes:

> They found — and made — much life, if only for a short while, as we have seen. Once sailors got, as Walter Kennedy put it, "the choice in themselves" — that is, the autonomous power to organize the ship and its miniature society as they wanted — they built a better world than the one they had found on the merchant, naval,

and privateering ships of the early modern Atlantic. They transformed harsh discipline into a looser, more libertarian way of running their ship that depended on "what Punishment the Captain and Majority of the Company shall think fit." They transformed the realities of chronically meager rations into riotous chronic feasting, an exploitative wage relation into a collective risk bearing, and injury and premature death into health care and security. Their democratic election of officers stood in stark, telling contrast to the near-dictatorial arrangement of command in the merchant service and Royal Navy.... These signs of life flowered in the black shadow of death, for if the dangers of the common seaman's life were extreme, those surrounding the pirate, in battle, in prison, or on the gallows, loomed even larger. They looked this grim reality in the eye and laughed.[10]

Roberts was not in a mood to laugh, however, as he contemplated his situation. He was now limited to a lightly gunned colonial sloop with forty men. The cargo, equipment, and resources of both the *Sagrada* and the *Royal Rover* were now lost to him. He had the leadership of a remaining knot of men who looked to him in large part to provide an answer to their dilemma. But they were, like Kennedy and his followers, men of extreme emotion and an inflamed lifestyle. Pirates were seen as "almost always mad or drunk" and they had an "unruly manner of living [that] was organized around the incessant use of strong drink. Drunkenness was so common among pirates that 'Sobriety brought a Man under a Suspicion of being in a Plot.'"[11] It must have been a daunting prospect. Turbulent men like pirates were not easy to lead.

It was difficult enough to find a way to govern men who had turned to piracy as a means of getting *away* from subordination, yet it was evident to Roberts and his remaining loyal men that some kind of agreed-upon arrangement to protect against internal lawlessness and treachery had to be found. As Stanley Richards wryly observes about Roberts's crew, the "strength of their company had previously been that of a rope of sand."[12]

Roberts's solution to their situation — as no doubt other pirate companies found — was to tell his forty men that future opportunities for plunder were still possible, but that their survival and success depended upon their accepting some kind of order or agreed principles that would govern them, and set rules for the common good, much in the manner of a medieval craft guild. In open session the men voted to accept the list of "Articles" that Roberts presented to them (summarized on pages 52–53), which addressed many issues of possible friction and had a whiff of democracy about them.

Later historians wondered if there were perhaps further articles, including Charles Johnson, who wrote:

> These, we are assured, were some of *Roberts's* Articles, but as they had taken Care to throw over-board the Original they had sign'd and sworn to, there is a great deal of Room to suspect, the remainder contained something too horrid to be disclosed to any, except such as were willing to be Sharers in the Iniquity of them.[13]

By the virtue or authority of these "Articles," horrid or not, the captain and the quartermaster were the leaders in the ship: the former to navigate and "fight" the ship, the latter to look after the seamen's rights and keep general order.

Having brought some discipline to his little command, Roberts faced the next order of business, which was to obtain provisions and supplies, the large part of the previous stocks having been carried off by Kennedy. It was voted to sail northeastward into the islands of the West Indies, where shipping was more active. Roberts apparently had some knowledge of the Leeward and Windward Islands, having spent some time there as mate of a Barbadian sloop. As Richards puts it, "he knew that area and its shipping; so now he had good cause to promise himself plentiful supplies from some hapless ships and an almost certain remedy for his misfortunes."[14]

The sloop was overcrowded and carried little armament, but the men had the weapons they had planned to use in taking the brigantine. Then, in an unexpected stroke of luck, a small pirate sloop, the *Sea King*, came along, and its captain, Montigny la Palisse, agreed that the little ships should sail together for mutual protection and profit. Optimistically renaming his sloop the *Fortune*, Roberts led the two vessels through the long, curving chain of islands, and kept watch for prey. It was now February 1720.

The initial landfalls produced little results, and Roberts kept the sloops on the windward or Atlantic side of the islands, with the steady southeast trade winds on his starboard quarter and the green and tan mounds of the island chain to leeward. Past the Grenadines, St. Lucia, Martinique, and the green gem of Dominica they sailed, until finally, off Deseada Island, which lies eastward off Guadeloupe, they pounced on three ships in

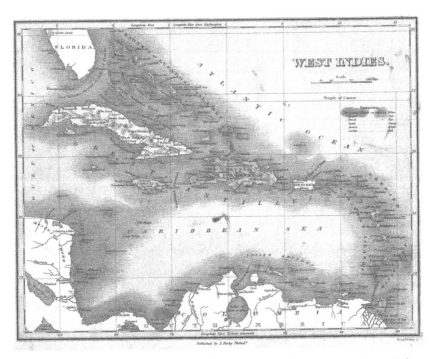

The Caribbean was the scene of Roberts's greatest overall success as a pirate. When he sailed south with two ships from Newfoundland in late 1720 he had become the most formidable fighting force to enter the West Indies. In a series of captures at sea and shore raids, he managed to bring West Indian trade to a standstill by spring 1721. He then left for West Africa and greater opportunity, never to return. In a twist of fate, his ships were brought back as prizes to Jamaica by Chaloner Ogle. One was sold, but Robert's old flagship, the Royal Fortune, *was destroyed by a great hurricane in the harbour of Port Royal.*

succession and looted them of basic stores, foodstuffs, and other prosaic needs of life, and possibly several ship's guns. With the two crews' spirits buoyed by these successes, Roberts then determined they should try for English shipping in other waters he knew well: those of Barbados.

Hovering off South Point, they saw a heavily laden vessel outbound from Bridgetown and Carlisle Bay and pounced on it. It proved to be a Bristol vessel of ten guns, and Roberts's men were thorough in their looting:

> From her they appropriated an abundance of clothes, some money, twenty-five bales of goods, five barrels of gunpowder, a cable, a hawser, ten casks of oatmeal, six casks of beef and many other articles, besides five men. They compelled the prize to stay put for three days, and on arrival [back] at Barbados she reported the matter to the Governor.[15]

The act of taking this Bristol vessel, however, set in motion a more robust response than Roberts had experienced from the Portuguese when he took the *Sagrada*. Governor Lowther of Barbados, on receiving the report from the Bristol vessel's captain, had no warship at his disposal, but instead commissioned a formidable little force to go out after Roberts. The *Summerset* galley of Bristol, carrying twenty guns and a crew of eighty, was joined by a ten-gun sloop, the *Philips*, with forty men. This little force was to be commanded by the captain of the galley, Rogers, under a governor's privateering commission, and it soon put to sea in search of Roberts. Within two days of clearing Bridgetown harbour, two strange sails were seen to the southwest, standing briskly in toward the Barbados ships. Roberts had not been able to resist what appeared to be two likely prizes.

Rogers played a canny game with Roberts, as the *Fortune*, followed by *Sea King*, came bowling along on reaches before the Trades to the attack. Rogers had the galley and sloop remain on course under easy sail, with men hidden and no evident commotion.

Thinking the capture of these ships would be easy, Roberts closed to musket-shot distance and fired a warning gun, expecting the vessels would let fly sheets, round up into the wind, and meekly await instructions. But, as Charles Johnson relates, the response was quite otherwise, and left Roberts with a lifetime animosity toward Barbados and Barbadians.

> The *Barbadoes* Ships kept an easy sail till the Pyrates came up with them, and then *Roberts* gave them a Gun, expecting they would have immediately struck to his piratical Flag, but instead thereof, he was forced to receive the Fire of a Broadside, with three Huzzas at the same Time; so that an Engagement ensued, but *Roberts* being hardly put to it, was obliged to crowd all the Sail the Sloop would bear, to get off: The Galley sailing pretty well, kept Company for a long while, keeping a constant Fire, which gall'd the Pyrate; however, at length by throwing over their Guns, and other heavy Goods, and thereby light'ning the Vessel, they, with much ado, got clear; but Roberts could never endure a *Barbadoes* Man afterwards, and when any Ship belonging to that Island fell in his Way, he was more particularly severe to them than others.[16]

It was a stinging defeat, for Roberts's crew had suffered half his men killed by the murderous fire from the galley, and he had lost his guns and many stores. To add bitterness, Montigny la Palisse had fled the scene as soon as it was evident the Barbados ships meant to fight. With his little ship damaged, with no guns, weed-fouled, and undermanned, and the sour taste of humiliation in his mouth, Roberts steered *Fortune* west before the wind to find shelter in the long chain of the Leeward Islands, and soon came up on the emerald green shores of Dominica.

Careful not to disturb the islanders, Roberts used the looted goods *Fortune* still carried from its captures to barter for food and other provisions, and managed to get his water casks filled. Almost as important, thirteen English seamen who had been stranded on the island by a French guard-vessel out of Martinique volunteered to join Roberts's crew. Before long, *Fortune* was in reasonable shape to go to sea again, but Roberts had not found a secure cove to careen the sloop and clean the hull. This fact, and the crew's double difficulties of small supplies of rum, brandy, or wine, and even less of willing partners among the moral women of the island, led Roberts to decide to sail for the Grenadines, to the southward, where a careening could more secretly take place.

He was right to be cautious: the French community on Dominica had got word to the governor of Martinique of the pirates' presence, and that they were sailing for the Grenadines. The governor of Martinique began to prepare a force of armed sloops to sail in pursuit of them.

Roberts found a cove on Carriacou where he spent a week careening and cleaning *Fortune*, until finally the crew's complaints about the lack of drink and women in Carriacou led Roberts to give in — and perhaps to feel some unease — and put to sea again. His luck held this time, if by a hair, for the well-armed force of pursuing vessels sent by Martinique's governor arrived off Roberts's careening cove on Carriacou in the early morning light, just a few hours after Roberts had sailed. It was sheer luck, and Roberts would be unaware of it till later.

The close call with the Martinique force was more provident than Roberts could know, for had the heavily gunned island sloops caught the *Fortune* helpless in the Carriacou lagoon, the ship would either have been captured or destroyed, and Roberts and his men would have choked out their lives at the end of a gibbet rope on the Martinique shore. To Roberts, his piratical career was at a low, humiliating ebb: he had been betrayed; had lost his most important prize and his ship; had been defeated by colonial ships; and had fled with twenty men dead, his sloop damaged, and all his guns jettisoned over the side. He had little to show for his commitment to the "Sweet Trade." The winter of 1719–20 had not been profitable or successful, to put it mildly.

Whether by discussion with his crew or personal instinct, Roberts resolved to work their way north out of the now-alerted West Indies and see what could be gained by cruising the American coast. Here, some of the remaining goods not thrown over off Martinique could be sold or bartered for basic supplies, and unwary prizes might come their way. But he was also aware of a great gathering of able vessels and prime seamen, which, if he played his hand carefully and audaciously, might give him at last the guns, the ships, and the men he needed; not only to make his mark as a true pirate, but for revenge upon the hated men of Barbados who had inflicted on him such a stinging defeat.

That great gathering was the cod fishery off Newfoundland, in the waters of what ultimately would become Canada.

Although he did not know it, it was there that he would be transformed from a nondescript vagrant robber of the sea into the veritable king of the pirates; and when he sailed again southward out of those Canadian waters with his black ensign of revenge flying, it would put fear into the minds of Caribbean merchants and island governors alike, and bring West Indian trade to a bloody, fearful standstill.

There were two targets in Roberts's mind for revenge now, because he had learned of the Martinique governor's vigorous effort to pursue and destroy him, and of his narrow escape from Carriacou. Both Barbados, which had humiliated him, and Martinique were now in his sights for dark revenge, and he would have a new ensign made up to fly when he returned southward to claim that revenge: a black flag with a white seaman's figure standing with his feet on skulls, one skull above the letters *ABH*, the other above the letters *AMH*. These stood for "A Barbados Head" and "A Martinique Head." It would fly alongside his signature ensign of a seaman holding up an hourglass with the figure of Death. Roberts took deeply personally any insult or attempt to thwart his intentions, and was capable of harsh violence. He longed, it would appear, to inflict this violence on the leadership of those islands. And his chance would come, in full measure.[17]

The attractions, for Roberts, in the north were many, including the prospects of captures along the American coast, the securing of the always needed provisions, and, foremost, the great northern fishery. As Peter Earle observes:

> One major summer raiding area, as it was to be for the pirates of the Golden Age, was the Newfoundland Banks where huge fleets of fishermen spent the summer catching, splitting, drying and salting cod for the Catholic tables of the Mediterranean. The main attraction for the pirates, however, was not the fish but the fishermen,

some of the hardiest seamen in the world who, willingly or not, were added to the pirate crews.[18]

As the spring of 1720 advanced, Roberts steered his little *Fortune* northward along the English colonies of the Atlantic seaboard. Though able to carry ten guns, the sloop had not recovered long guns to replace those lost in the bloody escape from Barbados, and so how Roberts was able to survive and benefit from the northward voyage at first is unclear. He may, as mentioned, have managed to sell or barter some of his remaining booty ashore, as a number of unscrupulous colonial officials were happy to turn a blind eye and allow trade in pirated goods. Or he may have made some unrecorded captures. Whatever the results, Roberts came into the waters of Atlantic Canada in late spring, suddenly appearing off the historic fishing village of Canso, Nova Scotia. Some fifteen schooners and sloops of the New England fishing fleet were at anchor there, in the narrow anchorage between the mainland and Cape Ann Island, and Roberts swept in on them, using his few weapons and the element of surprise to take the vessels one by one. They offered no resistance. He thoroughly looted each one, and may have secured ship's guns from some. The record is not clear whether he confined his attack to the anchored vessels or attacked the little village over his several days' stay.

Roberts next steered *Fortune* up past the long, lobster-claw shape of Cape Breton Island and entered the Gulf of St. Lawrence, where, somewhere north of what would become Prince Edward Island, he captured in quick succession three French merchant vessels, and a heavily laden English vessel, as well. From these ships, it is likely he secured not only a wealth of provisions, but enough guns to restore *Fortune's* fighting ability.

But now would come the master stroke of audacity, mirroring the one he had pulled off in Brazil, that would give Roberts the ships, men, guns, and resources that would end forever his vagrant, small-scale sea robber days.[19]

The great prizes for northern pirates, as we have seen, were the ships and men of the Newfoundland fishery. There could be found over a thousand vessels crewed by prime seamen working from harbours along the south coast of Newfoundland.

Roberts crossed Cabot Strait and made landfall on the great island's rocky south coast, then worked eastward, rounding the southern tip of the Avalon Peninsula before moving carefully up its east coast to Ferryland. There, Roberts repeated his swooping attack technique from Canso, and captured a dozen fishing vessels, which were thoroughly looted. Flush with gear and provisions from these ships, but realizing the hardworking little *Fortune* needed a refit — and its crew some rest — Roberts steered south again around Cape Race and set a course westward for Trepassey, a long, deep harbour on the south coast of the Avalon Peninsula.

Trepassey Harbour lies at the end of a long entry leading in from Cape Pine into Trepassey Bay, it ends at a wider but less deep cove known as Mutton Bay, and beside it, behind Powles Head, the longer, thin arm of the harbour proper reaches in deeper to end at two smaller coves. Although a narrow waterway to work out of under sail or sweeps, it offered protection from almost any wind save a strong southwesterly blow. Roberts arrived off Trepassey Bay on June 21, 1720, and as he worked his way in past Cape Pine on his larboard side and Powles Head

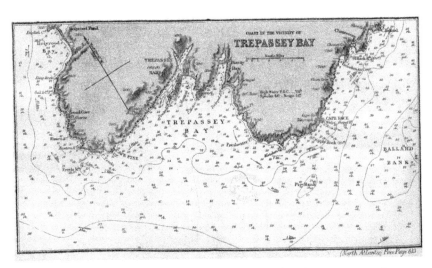

Trepassey, Newfoundland, was the scene of Roberts's transformation into the most formidable pirate of his day. On June 21, 1720, he surprised the anchored fishing fleet in the sheltered bay, capturing twenty-two ships and converting a frigate-sized ship into his new heavily armed flagship. From there, he would eventually leave Canadian waters to begin his extraordinary attack on West Indies trade.

ahead off his starboard bow, he could see no fewer than twenty-two ships were at anchor off the shore settlement. Ashore, some 150 smaller boats were drawn up, some under repair, others being readied for either the inshore fishery or the work on the Banks.

Roberts laid out his plan of attack, and to his astonished but likely gleeful crew it involved a full-on rush into the anchored formation, with every hand possible on deck to shout and threaten, the "Band of Musick" on deck drumming and tootling a lively and loud martial tune, guns fired in rapid succession off both sides of the sloop, and, aloft, English colours joined now by Roberts's rippling black pirate ensign. It was an appalling apparition, and even though the combined batteries of guns on the anchored ship numbered some forty, the crews who witnessed this terrifying entry fled ashore from their ships. In an audacious stroke of scarcely imaginable bravado, Roberts had become the master of twenty-two ships. It was an extraordinary act of daring, and it succeeded.[20]

With the place entirely in hand, Roberts summoned the captains of all twenty-two ships to daily meetings at which he demanded supplies or work and threatened to burn every vessel in the harbour unless he got them.

His stay stretched out into two plundering weeks, and four more merchant and fishing vessels that came in were immediately taken, as well. With now twenty-six ships to select from, Roberts chose a Bristol galley — one that could be rowed by great sweeps as well as sailed — of eighteen guns to be his new flagship, and shifted stores and guns into it. To this new ship of far greater power he gave the name *Royal Fortune*. His command now stood at two well-armed ships of ten and eighteen guns respectively.

What happened in detail during those two momentous weeks in Trepassey is subject to conjecture. One captive seaman, Moses Renos, who had been aboard the English vessel take in the Gulf of St. Lawrence, is said by historian Daniel Conlin to have written that Roberts "burned only a single ship, paid local carpenters for their work and bought — not stole — cannons and supplies from ashore" using money that the cash-poor fishermen were only too glad to accept.[21]

Charles Johnson, on the other hand, paints a far darker image of ruthless destruction and callous waste:

> It is impossible ... to recount the Destruction and Havock they made here, burning and sinking all the shipping, except a *Bristol* Galley, and destroying the Fisheries, and Stages of the poor Planters, without Remorse or Compunction; for nothing is so deplorable as Power in mean and ignorant Hands, it makes Men wanton and giddy, unconcerned at the Misfortunes they are imposing on their Fellow Creatures, and keeps them smiling at the Mischiefs, that bring themselves no Advantage. *They are like mad Men, that cast Fire-Brands, Arrows, and Death, and say, are not we in Sport?*[22]

The truth of Roberts's behaviour is uncertain. In many cases, it is impossible to be too harsh in judgment of pirates, yet Roberts revealed a strange mixture of consideration, even kindness, if Renos is to be believed, juxtaposed in the next moment with ruthless violence. This would increase now as his power increased, which the Trepassey Raid had given him immeasurably.

At the end of the two weeks, Roberts sailed eastward and north around Cape Spear again, and hovered off the mouth of St. John's Harbour, capturing a number of fishing vessels along the way. Conlin relates how Roberts took one vessel, the *Blessing*, which bestowed on *Royal Fortune* a new recruit of remarkable value:

> On board the pirates spotted a massive 20-year-old sailor named John Walden whom they forced to join them. Walden was soon nicknamed "Miss Nanny," in jest at his tough demeanour. Respected for his great strength he became, in the words of his shipmates, "a staunch Pyrate and great Rouge" who would fight with Roberts to the final battle. He could lift anchors and cut mooring cables with one blow and was usually sent

aboard captured ships with a poleaxe as the "key" to smash open locked doors and chests in search of loot.[23]

From the Avalon Peninsula, Roberts now steered southwest across Cabot Strait and coasted Cape Breton until he came to the waters off the new French-fortified harbour of Louisbourg, founded in 1713. It is not clear if Roberts penetrated the harbour — already protected by gun batteries — or whether he hovered to seaward off the port and picked off vessels as they left or returned, but he soon had taken, looted, and burned ten fishing vessels, saving only one, an excellent French full-rigged ship pierced for twenty-eight guns, of 220 tons, equivalent to a small naval frigate. This Louisbourg capture was too tempting to resist, and Roberts shifted himself and his crew to it, giving it now the *Royal Fortune* name. In a moment of characteristic consideration, the French vessel's prisoners were sent off safely in the eighteen-gun Bristol galley that had briefly been Roberts's flagship since Trepassey. But now, commanding what was in effect a twenty-eight-gun minor warship and an attendant and handy ten-gun sloop, Roberts steered southward into the waters off the Nova Scotian mainland, his mind set on not only the Banks fishing vessels, but, farther at sea, the steady procession of merchantmen following the Gulf Stream and the westerly winds for Europe, or beating in for Nova Scotia — newly won by the Treaty of Utrecht in 1713 — or for the Thirteen Colonies.

The captures came swiftly, and one of those captures, of the London ship *Samuel*, revealed not only the ferocious rapaciousness of the pirate crew, but also something of their fatalism. It was as if, as mentioned before, they knew at heart that they were dead men. As Johnson relates,

The *Samuel* was a rich Ship, and had several Passengers on board, who were used very roughly, in order to make them discover their Money, threatening them every Moment with Death, if they did not resign every Thing up to them. They tore up the Hatches and entered the Hold like a parcel of Furies, and with Axes and Cutlashes, cut and broke open all the Bales, Cases, and Boxes, they could lay their Hands on; and when any Goods came upon Deck, that they did not like to carry aboard, instead of tossing them into the Hold again, threw them over-board into the Sea; all this was done with incessant cursing and swearing, more like Fiends than Men. They carried with them, Sails, Guns, Powder, Cordage, and 8 or 9000 l. worth of the choicest Goods; and told Captain *Cary, That they should accept of no Act of Grace; that the K_____ and P_____t might be damned with their Acts of G_____ for them; neither would they go to Hope-Point, to be hang'd up a Sun drying, as Kidd's and Braddish's Company were; but that if they should ever be overpower'd, they would set Fire to the Powder, with a Pistol, and go all merrily to Hell together.*[24]

The captures kept coming apace as the Nova Scotian summer wore on: a Bristol snow; the *Little York* of Virginia, the *Love* of Liverpool, the *Phoenix* of Bristol, an unnamed brigantine, all of whose crew were pressed into pirate service and the ships sunk; *Sudbury*, a sloop; the list goes on. But Roberts was aware that the summer would soon come to an end and his preoccupation was with a return from the cold waters of Nova Scotia to the warm climes of the West Indies — but now formidably armed to avenge the humiliations of before and emboldened by his power.

He sailed south, out of the northern waters of the future Canada, where he had been transformed by audacity and luck, his black flag now streaming confidently aloft, for the destiny that awaited him in tropic waters.

His pursuit of that destiny would strike Caribbean merchants and governors with a thunderbolt of violence that would appall them, and would render Roberts the acknowledged king of the Atlantic pirates for a brief, incandescent few months. He had entered the waters of the future Canada virtually another luckless brigand; he was leaving them a ferociously successful pirate commander of a flotilla of ominous force. In an uncanny way, this Welshman had undergone a transformation in Canadian waters as profound in some ways as that which occurred to another seaman, in character as unlike him as it was possible to be: the Yorkshireman James Cook, who entered Canadian waters an undistinguished Royal Navy warrant officer and left them the renowned "Surveyor of the Fleet" that took Wolfe to Quebec, bound for three voyages of Pacific discovery. For Cook, the transformation happened through hard work, exceptional diligence, and devotion to duty. For Roberts, it came through discipline, audacity, cunning ruthlessness, ability, and the recovery of nerve and confidence shaken in the distant Caribbean. More than either man would ever know, it was the waters of Canada that made them, and handed them their destinies.

7

A Grim Vengeance

As Roberts's powerful little flotilla left Canadian waters at the end of that transformative summer, they reached south across the westerly winds into the turbulent waters of the Gulf Stream, with Roberts steering a course for Deseada Island, off Guadeloupe's east coast. There he proposed to wait, as the pirates jokingly said, for goods "consigned to them." There may have been more business than bravado in that statement, for there was some suspicion at the time that pirate flotillas, by prior arrangement, may have received supplies at sea from merchants, or colonial administrators, not overly worried where profit could be found.

> And it has been very much suspected that Ships have loaded with Provisions at the *English* Colonies, on pretence of Trading on the Coast of *Africa*, when they have in reality been consigned to [the pirates]; and tho' a shew of Violence is offered to them when they meet, yet they are pretty sure of bringing their Cargo to a good Market.[1]

Whether Roberts had entered into such an arrangement is not known, but it is doubtful; there was too much of the lone outsider in him. And there had been a change in his demeanour, as well; whether from the need to command sizeable ships and scores of men with an air of detached authority, or from an evolution in his own personality, Roberts had become a far more stern, remote figure. He now had a willingness to act with ruthless violence against those who opposed him, and was less likely to limit his men in their own violence. He had taken to dressing grandly in breeches, waistcoat, and coat of scarlet velvet when an attack was to be made, slung about with pistols on silken lanyards. As he was tall, darkly handsome, "of good parts," and physically strong after a life at sea, he must have presented an imposing figure. To his men he brought the value of being a proven, cunning, and courageous fighter, and to that point a successful navigator, but there was now a restrained formality to his ways, masking either motives of leadership or others difficult to discern.

More and more evident, too, with each capture, was Roberts's sharing with his men the sense of exacting "justice" on behalf of oppressed seamen from tyrannical masters, perhaps drawing on his own experiences. It became a hallmark of their capture routine, as Rediker observes:

> Upon seizing a merchantman, pirates often administered the "Distribution of Justice," "enquiring into the Manner of the Commander's Behaviour to their Men, and those, against whom Complaint was made" were "whipp'd and pickled" ... Bartholomew Roberts's crew considered such inquiry so important that they formally designated one of their men, George Willson, as the "Dispencer of Justice."[2]

Captured captains of whom their crews spoke well were often, in contrast, treated handsomely to dinner by Roberts, and could find their ships and all or part of the cargos they carried returned to them. Conversely, captains complained about as cruel brutes by their men could themselves be subjected to horrifying cruelties from Roberts's men, which Roberts did little or nothing to prevent.

Having taken in stores by various means at Deseada, Roberts now convinced his crews that an eastward passage to West Africa would prove the most profitable, and the ships turned their jib-booms toward the distant Cape Verde Islands, where Roberts hoped to water and replenish the ships for the next track southeast to the slaving ports.

Although Roberts had until this point demonstrated competence in navigation, it was in itself an inexact science in 1720. The principle, as mentioned earlier, was "lead, latitude, and lookout," and that meant sounding for the bottom, sailing east or west along a line of latitude, found most easily by the noon sun sight or by observing the North Star's altitude above the horizon — at least as far as the Equator, when it dipped into the northern horizon — and watching for the desired landfall before running into it.

To reach the Cape Verdes, which lie off what is now Senegal, would mean a long tack into the southeast trades, as much along the line of fifteen degrees north latitude as possible. The square rigs of his ships made windward work difficult under any circumstance, and after a long passage Roberts brought his ships to within lookouts' sighting of the misty, distant island peaks, but his ships were too far to leeward to have a hope of beating up to them. It was a bitter setback, as much caused by the limitations of early-eighteenth-century ship rigs and winds as any miscalculation on Roberts's part — he had held a correct course for the islands — but he had no choice but to wear about and run for the South American coast before the Trades, hoping they would make landfall before their rapidly diminishing stores and water ran out. It would be a near run thing, in any event, being a voyage of more than two thousand miles. The passage across westward was nearly fatal: they eventually had but one hogshead of water to serve more than 120 men in both ships. That water ran out, and as Johnson relates, disaster loomed:

> They continued their Course, and came to an Allowance of one single Mouthful of Water for 24 Hours; many of them drank their Urine, or Sea Water, which instead of allaying, gave them an inextinguishable Thirst, that killed them: Others pined and wasted a little more Time in Fluxes and Apyrexies [diarrhea and fever], so that they dropped away daily: Those that sustain'd the Misery best, were such as almost starved themselves, forbearing

all Sorts of Food, unless a Mouthful or two of Bread the whole Day, so that those who survived were as weak as it was possible for Men to be and alive.[3]

With little method to determine longitude, Roberts had resorted to heaving to at night to avoid running aground once he sensed the South American coast was close: by luck, one such night the leadsman reported seven fathoms of water, and they anchored, finding in the morning that land was visible, but at a great distance. A boat was sent away, and managed to struggle back that night with not only a life-saving supply of water, but the news that Roberts had brought them, almost ironically, to a familiar coast: the mouth of the Maroni River on the Suriname coast. It was just west of Devil's Island and the Suriname River where Kennedy had betrayed him, seemingly so long ago.

With water, but still without sufficient food or other supplies, Roberts steered the ships toward the latitude of Barbados, to intercept shipping bound there or for the Leeward Islands. They quickly made several captures, and soon had secured not only the needed replenishment but also more men to replace those who had died on the disastrous Cape Verde voyage. More captures followed, including no less than five heavily laden ships from the Virginia coast. But Roberts found his ships were sluggish, and decided to careen them to clear the fouling from the Atlantic crossings. He turned again to the same cove at Carriacou, where he had learned in detail of the Martinique force sent against him and which he had escaped by luck on sailing for the American coast.

Roberts's flotilla arrived at Carriacou on September 4, 1720, and there he stayed, careening his ships while his men used the longboat to pounce on island boats, stealing turtles and other goods. Over their three weeks there, the assembled company voted that easy pickings seemed at hand in the Caribbean, and the Africa voyage was set aside for the time being.

While at Carriacou, Roberts learned that the governor at Basseterre on St. Christopher (now St. Kitts), Lieutenant-General William Mathew, had either ordered or been responsible in some way for the execution of pirates on the nearby island of Nevis. At the end of September, Roberts steered *Royal Fortune* and *Fortune* for Basseterre. When they arrived, they entered with Roberts's by now customary display of black ensigns, ringing gunfire, and a band of musicians gamely blaring away on deck. The results were as dramatic as the entrance: virtually everything afloat in the harbour struck its colours and Roberts began a selective looting of them while sending a boat ashore with a somewhat more prosaic villainy in mind: stealing some sheep.

Roberts retained one of the prizes, a vessel captained by a man named Fowles, and remained at anchor in the harbour while his men chased sheep ashore and the governor was feverishly gathering together militiamen and supplies of powder for the guns of the small fort. Roberts made no attempt to land the rest of his men, and the next morning the governor was at last able to mount a surprisingly credible defence. As Richards relates:

> The following morning the pirates were still lying off the Road, waiting to secure more sheep. About 11 o'clock, the *Fortune*, she that once had created havoc in Newfoundland, stood directly in and, when she approached the shipping, the shore battery opened up with thirteen big guns, including a 24-pounder, and fired two rounds. Seven shots hit her, tearing down her jib and cutting her halyards so that her mainsail settled, and it was suspected her bow was damaged. Not returning any fire, she faced about hurriedly and both pirate vessels ran into the Grand Golette where they cast Fowles' ship adrift. Failing to stretch away for the island of Nevis they headed westward close to the coast followed by about 70 horse and dragoons along the shore, and they were last seen to the north-east of St. Bartholomew's.[4]

Roberts, at some cost, had exacted some revenge for the execution of the pirates. Of interest, however, is that the attack did produce one of the few extant pieces of writing from Roberts, in the form of an oddly polite letter threatening Governor Mathew. Roberts had apparently invited Mathew out to share a drink in his flagship before the attack, and the man's refusal annoyed him considerably.

Royal Fortune,
Sept. 27th, 1720.

This comes expressly from me to lett you know that had you come off as you ought to a done, and drank a glass of wine with me and my company, I should not have harmed the least vessell in your harbour. Farther, it is not your gunns you fired that affrighted me or hindered our coming in shore, but the wind not proving to our expectation that hindered it. The *Royal Rover* you have already burnt and barbarously used some of our men, but we have now a ship as good as her, and for revenge you may assure yourselves, here and hereafter, not to expect anything from our hands but what belongs to a pirate. As farther, Gentlemen, that poor fellow you have in prison at Sandy Point is entirely ignorant and what he hath was gave him, and so prey make conscience for once, let me begg you, and use that man as an honest man and not as a [criminal]. If we hear any otherwise you may expect not to have quarters to any of your Island.

Yours,
Bathll. Roberts[5]

Given that Roberts was likely born and raised speaking only Welsh, the letter is remarkably articulate and reveals a man of touchy sensitivity and a firm belief of his equality with those in authority. If St. Kitts had proven an unpleasant experience, the island of St. Bartholomew proved anything but. The French governor had decided that discretion was the better part of valour, and Roberts and his crew were pleased to be warmly welcomed ashore. The pirate ships were victualled and supplied, and social functions ashore and the warm attentions of the island women made up handsomely for the ill treatment at St. Kitts: "Roberts' men, for instance, had handsome treatment at the hands of St. Bartholomew, where the women endeavoured to attract the good graces of such generous lovers, that paid well for their favours."[6]

After several luxurious weeks at St. Bartholomew, Roberts got a vote to put the flotilla to sea again, as he was anxious to get back to the "Sweet Trade," if only to replenish depleted coffers. By the end of October 1720, he was prowling the waters off St. Lucia, capturing ships at an alarming rate: in one three-day period, he took no fewer than fifteen English and French ships. The reputation of Roberts was growing as the winter wore on, so that frantic letters from worried planters, merchants, and island governors began to refer to him as the "Great Pirate Roberts."

It did not always mean plunder without cost, however. Some ships chose to fight back, and incurred a ferocious response from the pirates, whom Roberts could not have restrained had he wished to. And through it all there burned a hot flame of animosity from Roberts toward the islands of Martinique and Barbados. As David Cordingly relates:

> Bartholomew Roberts was merciless in his treatment of seamen from Martinique or Barbados because the governors of those islands had made various attempts to capture him. In 1721 he raided shipping off Martinique and captured their crews. According to the report sent to London on February 18, 1721, "Some they almost whipped to death, others had their ears cut off, others they fixed to the yard arms and fired at them as a mark." In [January] 1721 Roberts endeavored to board a Dutch ship anchored at St. Lucia. The crew tried to prevent the attack by running out booms and fenders, and then opened fire. For nearly four hours they fought off the pirates and killed a great number of them. When the Dutch ship was at length overpowered, the pirates were ruthless in revenging the death of their comrades, and slaughtered any man they found alive.[7]

The Dutch vessel, which bore the name *El Puerto del Principe*, was fitted with thirty guns. Against that firepower were *Royal Fortune's* thirty-two guns and the smaller vessel's eighteen. The *Principe* made a handsome addition to the flotilla, if dearly bought, and Roberts had its damage repaired and increased its total of guns to thirty-six.

Using the Dutch vessel, Roberts then sailed it up to Martinique, cruising the coast with a pre-arranged signal flying that he had learned the Dutch used to signal Martinique smugglers that trade awaited off St. Lucia. The bait worked, and as Roberts and his ships hid behind green headlands, Martinique trading sloops and schooners sailed south, only to fall into Roberts's trap. Fourteen ships and boats were taken and looted of money and provisions, then all were burned save one, which was sent back to Martinique crammed with the captured crews and news of Roberts's developing revenge against the island.[8]

By this point, Roberts was flying the two colours that had become his trademark: the black ensign with the sailor and Death holding aloft an hourglass, and the newer "Revenge" ensign of the sailor figure standing atop two skulls. He was rapidly becoming the undisputed master of the Caribbean Sea, and trade was beginning to wither badly as a result. Things were not far from coming to a crisis point for commerce in the islands.

With the Dutch vessel now part of his fleet, Roberts stered to the north-west ahead of the Trades; he needed a safe port to let his wounded heal, to careen and repair his ships, and to respond to the entreaties of his crews, who were clamouring for women, jollity ashore, and drink — the last being lost somewhat on Roberts, who seems never to have drunk anything more potent than tea.

Again, with commendable navigational skill, Roberts brought his ill-disciplined and ragged little fleet to the safe harbour of Bahia de Samana, on the great island of Hispaniola, now the location of Haiti and the Dominican Republic. There, he shifted his fleet about: the little sloop *Fortune* that had carried him to greatness in Newfoundland, he burned, moving its crew to the brigantine taken so long before off Devil's Island. He renamed that ship *Good Fortune* — it appears to have served as a stores ship for the *Royal Fortune* throughout. The brigantine's crew and captain were moved into the Dutch vessel.

Providentially, while entering Hispaniola's waters, Roberts had taken a handsome French frigate, which Roberts kept, transferring the name *Royal Fortune* to it and giving the old *Royal Fortune*, taken in Canadian waters, to the French captain and crew in compensation. If these constantly changing ship arrangements are confusing to the modern reader, one can only imagine how difficult it was to keep track of in the eighteenth century.

One person was not so lucky: it was the governor of Martinique, aboard the French vessel for some reason. Roberts had him run up by the neck on a rope attached to the French ship's yardarm. As the governor kicked out his life in slow strangulation, the death completed the greater part of the round of grim vengeance Roberts had sought to achieve.

The panic that Roberts's activities were causing in the Caribbean had spread to the American mainland, particularly after Governor Spotswood of Virginia learned Roberts was swearing revenge against the colony for several pirates recently hung there. Roberts had stopped a vessel that was northbound to Virginia precisely to have it convey a warning that he was coming in to exact that vengeance.

Spotswood had sufficient information to know that Roberts was strong enough to carry out his threat. He sprang into action, particularly when the commander of the Royal Navy vessel on station, the *Rye*, quietly observed that he would be overwhelmed by Roberts's force. Spotswood established gun batteries at numerous coastal locations and wrote to other colonial governors asking that any Royal Navy assets on their shores be sent to Virginian waters. Historian Donald Shomette reveals the sense of panic:

> Governor Alexander Spotswood's anxiety intensified when word arrived informing him that Roberts had captured a French warship with the governor of the island of Martinique aboard. It was said the rovers had proceeded to hang the unfortunate Frenchman from the yardarm. Others aboard had their ears sliced off or were tied to the yardarm and used for [shooting] practice.[9]

Spotswood was hearing tales that combined Roberts's actions off St. Lucia and the frigate capture; nonetheless, his preparations for Roberts's attack continued. The Spanish governors on Hispaniola, however, were welcoming to Roberts and his men when they found out they were there; women flooded to the ships and shore camp, drawn by the lure of gold, and the pirates were free to enter into a prolonged period of drinking and orgiastic debauchery that caused previous such activity to pale in comparison.

Roberts remained aloof, a strange, distant figure, never straying from his abstemious personal habits as regards drink or women, yet unconcerned — or unable to alter — that his men shared little or none of his restraint. The roots of this reticence may have lain in his Welsh village upbringing, or in his psychological or sexual nature: the answer is unknown. He was nonetheless a model of leadership and efficiency while his men immersed themselves in drunken excess, managing to find enough sober hands to get his ships provisioned and careened and their gear readied again for sea, all the while considering the reality of his situation. The few ships of the Royal Navy in the Caribbean had so far skilfully managed to avoid confronting him, and the azure seas of the Caribbean were his to control — for now. He knew it could not last. As Stanley Richards observes:

> By the Spring of 1721 Black Bart had brought sea-borne trade in the West Indies practically to a standstill. So there was no point in investing the shipping for further plunder. His own two vessels were full of plundered goods for which he wanted gold, but he was not prepared to court disaster on the American seaboard in trading his goods. He knew that his enemies were on the alert for him, and he realized the possibility of being caught in an unguarded moment whilst trading, especially as his men were prone to roistering when ashore. On consulting his House of Lords it was agreed to depart from the Americas, the House of Commons apparently falling in with the decision.

Roberts had ranged [in the Caribbean] freely for over a year, and although the Royal Navy had avoided battle with him he guessed that a joint expedition of more than one navy would ultimately be sent against him since he had openly defied and abused the accredited representatives of both the British and French Crowns. As a matter of fact, the Governor of the Leeward Islands demanded that resolute action by men-of-war be taken against "the great pirate Roberts" who took ships as he willed.[10]

Accordingly, at the beginning of April 1721, Bartholomew Roberts, master of the Caribbean Sea, turned the jib-booms of his ships eastward. Once more, they would attempt the crossing to West Africa, and the riches of the slave trade. Roberts would not see West Indian waters again. His fate lay in the waters off Africa, far across the Atlantic Ocean.

8

Plunder and Loot

A s Roberts turned the prows of his ships eastward toward Africa, he was leaving a Caribbean Sea where the ineptitude of national navies to deal with the pirate menace had been thoroughly demonstrated by his own success. Historian Peter Earle has observed that not only did pirates have a better knowledge of the waters and islands, being at sea almost all the time while the navy remained in port, but in the 1720s "the Navy never did get the right mix of a few powerful ships to overawe the really strong pirates and large numbers of small, fast and light-draft frigates and sloops equipped with oars to catch the rest."[1]

Pirates were making impossible the establishment of long-term, profitable Caribbean trade after the end, in 1713, of the wars with Louis XIV and the brief interruption of naval protection caused by the 1718–1720 War of the Quadruple Alliance. In 1721, as Roberts set out for Africa, the very agitated Governor Spotswood of Virginia was again informing the board of trade "that in his opinion there were no ships of war in all America that were individually strong enough to take on a pirate force of the likes or strength of a Bartholomew Roberts." Roberts was king of those waters indeed.[2]

The problem was compounded by the ponderous performance of British warships — one observer was famously quoted as saying they were built by the mile and cut off as required — and the difficulties they had in catching the fleet pirate vessels. Admiral Edward Vernon was known to have remarked that dispatching a large naval vessel after a pirate ship was akin to sending "a Cow after a Hare."[3] Further, Royal Navy ships were fully manned only during wartime, and the pursuit of pirates usually occurred in peacetime, when naval vessels might carry a third less men, in contrast to the heavily populated pirate ships. The voluble Spotswood demanded that the naval vessels on his coasts have their full complements, "for that," as he grumbled, "in these parts it is, in a manner, open war, the coasts being daily infested by pirates."[4]

There was another factor in the business, which was somewhat embarrassing to the navy:

> The pirates' penchant for terror even seems to have had an intimidating effect on the officers and sailors of the British Royal Navy. From 1717 onward colonial officials and merchants voiced a chorus of complaints that His Majesty's Ships seemed none too eager to engage the freebooters who were so dramatically disrupting trade. Merchants especially grumbled that naval vessels would rather trade than fight pirates.[5]

The Royal Navy's reluctance to fight the pirates ship on ship (Maynard's killing of Blackbeard in 1718 was an exception) had a degree of common sense to it, when one considers that Roberts's flagship, the *Royal Fortune*, carried 128 men and bristled with eighteen 8-pounder guns, four 12-pounders, twelve 6-pounders, eight 4-pounders, and a clutch of smaller guns and swivels. As discussed earlier, a gun was classified by the weight of cast-iron ball it fired. The little consort brigantine, *Good Fortune*, meant to be a stores ship, was astonishingly packed with no less than 140 men and carried six 6-pounders and six 2-pounders, plus a plethora of small arms and assorted cutlery.[6]

In exasperation, as Rediker observes, the British authorities attempted to harden the anti-pirate legal environment:

English imperial rulers toughened the law of piracy in 1721 ... promising death to anyone who cooperated with pirates and the loss of wages and six months' imprisonment to those who refused to defend their ship. They also decreed that naval ships were not to trade but to chase and fight pirates, which they had shown considerable disinclination to do, much to the dismay of both merchants and royal officials. Seamen injured in battle against pirates "shall be provided for as if they were actually in the service of the Crown," explained the *Boston News-Letter.*[7]

Whatever the actions to oppose him, Bartholomew Roberts steered away from the inert wreckage of the Caribbean trading network, intent now on plundering what he could from the cluster of ships whose work he knew well — the slaving vessels that had been his own world a few years previously. But opposition suddenly faced him from within his own ranks.

As Roberts had moved from success to success, his crews began in some quarters to see him as aloof and arrogant, behaviour that easily touched pirates' hair-trigger sensitivity. Finally, an event occurred at the beginning of the eastward Atlantic passage that seemed to bear them out.

A drunken seaman had insulted Roberts to his face, and Roberts drew a pistol and shot the man dead on the spot. The victim had a close friend in the pirate company, a hulking young Welshman named Thomas Jones. Jones confronted Roberts in a rage, and Roberts responded by drawing his sword and attempting to run the giant through. Jones responded by pummelling Roberts with his fists. When the quartermaster saw that Roberts, no weakling himself, was bent over a gun and getting the worst of the brutal fist fight, he halted the affair. Jones was dragged off Roberts and sent below, where he nursed his grievance and found allies in many of the crew, including the captain of the stores ship brigantine, a man named Anstis.

On a dark night, as the ships worked eastward away from the Leeward Islands, Anstis and Jones — who had moved to the brigantine — made their move, and *Good Fortune* dropped away without notice, turning back for the Caribbean. Roberts found an empty horizon when he came on deck in the morning: *Royal Fortune* would go on to Africa alone.[8]

This time, the eastward passage to the African coast was achieved without incident, and the *Royal Fortune* made landfall on June 12, 1721, off the mouth of the Senegal River, where an important French trading and slave post stood to deal not only in slaves but gumwood. Two French guard ships came out to challenge Roberts, but upon Roberts opening his gun ports and hoisting his black ensign, both ships immediately surrendered.

In a stroke, Roberts had regained a flotilla. The larger vessel, the *Comte de Thoulouze*, of sixteen guns, was refitted, mounted with twenty-four guns and renamed *Ranger*, while the smaller ship, the *Ste. Agnes*, was turned into a stores ship and named *Little Ranger*. This work presumably went on while the ships procured provisions ashore somehow: the record is not clear.[9]

Roberts then sailed his flotilla along the coast toward the mouth of the Sierra Leone River, word of his arrival passing quickly — one wonders how — and adding to the consternation of the merchants and traders, who since 1719 had endured swarms of pirates operating on the Guinea coast, to the point that in two years, pirates had taken almost one hundred ships.

Arriving at a cove near the river mouth, later named Pirates' Bay, Roberts effortlessly took six more prizes he found at anchor there. Roberts had a memory of Sierra Leone from his days with Howell Davis: the private merchants ashore could be friendly if handled correctly. There was a proper beach for careening, water, wood, and victuals could be got — and the African women proved welcoming to pirates who had coin in hand.

When Roberts and his men finally went ashore in force they were welcomed by traders who had dealt happily with Davis, and the crews joyfully gave themselves over to six weeks of debauchery and drink, the looting of their captured prizes, and a leisurely careening of their ships.[10]

One incident revealed a side to Roberts's character not usually in evidence: humour and an agreeable humanity. The Royal Africa Company had a small, ineffective fort on Bence Island, at the mouth of the river. Roberts attacked it after resistance had been offered by its governor, a man named Plunkett. When Plunkett was taken after the fort was easily overwhelmed with little loss, he was brought before Roberts. The original account of their meeting, as cited by Marcus Rediker, went as follows:

> [U]pon the first sight of Plunkett [Roberts] swore at him like any Devil, for his Irish Impudence in daring to resist him. Old Plunkett, finding he had got into bad Company, fell a swearing and cursing as fast or faster than Roberts; which made the rest of the Pirates laugh heartily, desiring Roberts to sit down and hold his Peace, for he had no Share in the Pallaver with Plunkett at all. So that by meer Dint of Cursing and Damning, Old Plunkett ... sav'd his life.[11]

More ominous for Roberts was the news that a powerful Royal Navy force had recently been at Sierra Leone. It had been sent out to Africa in June 1720 after the Royal Africa Company made a desperate plea to the Admiralty. But this was not a clutch of hesitant sloops-of-war with timid captains overawed by Roberts's strength. The Admiralty had sent the fifty-gun, fourth-rate line battleship *Swallow*, under Chaloner Ogle, and the similar fifty-gun *Weymouth*, under Captain Mungo Herdman.

Ogle was the senior of the two, and was serving as commodore. The ships had sailed from Sierra Leone at the end of April and had promised to return to the river by Christmas. Roberts now had a new factor in the equation of his raiding: no longer was he sure of being the most powerful force on the coast. A serious threat was posed to his movements. By the end of July 1721, Roberts determined the flotilla had to sail, for word had come that the voluble Plunkett had managed to alert the distant warships of Roberts's presence and had sent off a petition to London asking that the Ogle's ships stay on the coast until the threat was dealt with. It was the first sign that the power of government was beginning slowly to draw a noose around Roberts's neck.[12]

With this sailing, Roberts entered the last six months of his career, and his life. And almost as if he sensed the approach of Fate, the pace of activity in his flotilla and crews began to increase. But now there were instances of cruelty and diversion from the carefully planned "Articles" that had given Roberts and his crews such cohesion on their emergence south out of Canadian waters, where the transformation into power had taken place.

The scene for this last great act of Roberts's career was the long half-circle of African coastline that began above where Liberia now is, round to the long, eastward-leading shores of what were then known as the Ivory Coast, the Gold Coast, and the Slave Coast, and then into the fever-ridden coves of the Bight of Benin, where the coastline turned southward again and led along what was called Lower Guinea to the prominent Cape Lopez, virtually on the equator. Off that Lower Guinea coast lay the line of islands that, as we have seen, figured in Roberts's initial piratical career, when he adopted the life. These were, again, Fernando Po; Principe, or Prince's Island; São Tomé; and Annobón, stretching in a line to the southwest. Over all these fetid, fever-ridden coasts the prevailing winds were the Trades, making westward runs fairly simple but eastward voyaging more difficult. It was much because of the latter that Roberts concentrated the plundering and action of the winter of 1721–22 in the easternmost waters, so that he would have the windward position should the heavy warships he now knew were hunting him attempt to find him — which they did.

As Roberts began to prey upon the slave trade ships and the merchantmen that supported the shore establishments, his new ruthlessness became more evident, inspired perhaps by his deep hatred of the brutal ways of slave-trading captains toward slave and sailor alike; a possible legacy of his own career as a slaver. He became more insistent that the crew carry out the bloody ritual of "Distribution of Justice" mentioned earlier, which now involved dispensing a fearful lashing to any captain whose sailors complained of his treatment. One senses a greater darkness entering Roberts's spirit and soul, as if proximity again to the inhuman

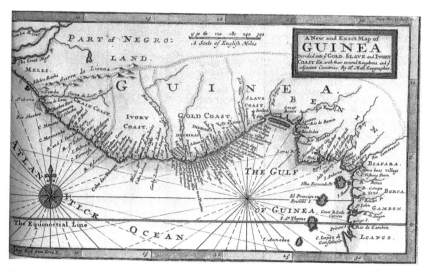

Herman Moll (1654?–1732) was a Dutch cartographer who relocated to London in 1730. His map shows the great curved stretch of coast where Roberts first entered the African pirate world, and where, off Cape Lopez, he left it at the hands of Chaloner Ogle.

practice of slavery was bringing out passions he had not shown so readily in his western Atlantic career.[13]

After a brief voyage to Prince's Island to replenish his supplies, Roberts had sailed a broad reach into the mainland coast to Sestos, in modern Liberia, before turning to begin beating his way eastward to prey on the shipping inshore. Off Sestos he immediately had the good fortune to intercept a fine new twenty-six-gun frigate of the Royal Africa Company, the *Onslow*, outbound for the major RAC post at Cape Coast Castle, hundreds of leagues farther east along the Gulf of Guinea coast. On August 8, 1721, Roberts forced *Onslow* to heave to, and in a remarkably civilized process, negotiated an exchange of ships with *Onslow's* captain, Michael Gee. Roberts received *Onslow*, and in turn gave his French-built *Royal Fortune* to Gee. The RAC ship went through a rebuilding process — one wonders where — that saw it metamorphose into a powerful forty-gun ship, altered to make it a formidable adversary indeed.

As Charles Johnson explains,

The Pyrates kept the *Onslow* for their own Use, and gave Captain *Gee* the *French* Ship, and then fell to making such Alterations as might fit her for a Sea-Rover, pulling down her Bulk-Heads, and making her flush, so that she became, in all Respects, as compleat a Ship for their Purpose, as any they could have found; they continued to her the Name of the *Royal Fortune*, and mounted her with 40 Guns.[14]

On capturing the ship, Roberts noted that a number of men clearly looked as if they wanted to join the pirates, but were fearful of openly volunteering. Seeing their "Petitioning Countenance," Roberts made it easy for them, saying "I must oblidge these Fellows with a Shew of force."[15]

Although Roberts had acted with surprising consideration with regard to the would-be recruits, he showed again a departure from previous rules by allowing an Englishwoman outbound to join her husband at Cape Coast Castle to be kept aboard rather than be sent off with Captain Gee. A seaman appointed to "protect" her would later boast loudly on the gallows that he had been her lover, even as she stood in the audience watching his execution. Unlike some pirate captains who treated women with brutality, Roberts seems never to have permitted callous cruelty toward them, although his general tolerance of savagery seems to be evident in these last months.

The warships *Swallow* and *Weymouth* were at this time "upwind" in the theatre, having worked their way up to Prince's Island, where they undoubtedly learned of Roberts's recent visit. Whether Roberts in turn was aware of their location or simply operated on his instincts, he had his flotilla cruise offshore as it tacked eastward along the Guinea coast, flying French colours until it drew closer to the infamous Bight of Benin, and he put in to Jacquin, the principal slaving port of the African kingdom of Allada. Their stay there was brief, as there is the suggestion that Roberts's crews had been weakened by deadly fever. The saying at the time went "Beware and take care / Of the Bight of Benin / For one that comes out / There were forty went in." No figures exist on Roberts's crew losses by fever, but it is logical they were many.[16]

If Jacquin or other Slave Coast ports were deadly to European seamen, the next landfall was even more so, as they steered into the "elbow" of the coast and a smaller bay called the Bight of Biafra, seeking the trading posts — and the ships visiting them — at the mouth of the Calabar River. It was here they arrived at the beginning of October 1721, and an insalubrious destination it proved to be, as Richards relates:

> Staying but briefly at Jacquin they pressed on for Old Calabar in the Bight of Biafra, in the eastern corner of what is now Nigeria. It is about the most unhealthy spot on the Coast, with its malaria, yellow and blackwater fevers, and the innumerable diseases caused by insects, worms, etc. The climate is muggy in the extreme and steamy-hot for most of the year. Calabar was, however, a place quite suitable for careening. To enter the river there is a bar, in those days drawing no more than 13 feet of water. The river-channels meander through a labyrinth of creeks, so that it would have been difficult for a man-of-war to attack them there.[17]

Roberts forced a captured captain to act as a pilot and took his ships well up into the creeks, so as not to be seen from seaward. Then, using ship's boats, they descended the river to pounce on arriving vessels. By this surprising means, they captured four English vessels, which were thoroughly looted. The pirate crews had expected to obtain provisions — and access to women — with ease, idling in the stifling heat in an alcoholic haze when not careening a ship or looting a capture. But the local population refused to deal with them, and when Roberts sent ashore an armed party of forty men to force access to resources, they were astonished to find a formidable body of two thousand men gathered to oppose them. The pirates showed remarkable resolution under the circumstances, pressing forward even after several of them had been felled by hurled spears, and this courage plus the superior weaponry the pirates handled with great effectiveness caused the Africans to lose their nerve, break, and run. Roberts's men then ended any further chance of remaining on the Calabar by burning the inhabitants' villages.

No further contact with the people was possible, but that also meant no provisioning. Finishing the careening as soon as he could, Roberts ordered the flotilla to work out of the creeks and out into the open sea — likely with relief — and they turned southward toward Cape Lopez, where they managed to take on fresh water before crossing westward to the island of Annobón, last in the chain, for provisions.

There, rumours were flying about the warships: they were at Sierra Leone; they were laid up with crews decimated by fever; they were at Cape Coast Castle. The truth was uncertain.

Rather than flee the West African waters — the Caribbean always beckoned — Roberts made the fateful decision to sail north again, to the Ivory, Gold, and Slave coasts, and work an eastward coastal passage, plundering what shipping he found. He would take his chances of encountering the warships.

The track northward was uneventful, and the ships made landfall at Cape Lahou, on the Ivory Coast, and began to work eastward. The capture of a Dutch ship, the *Vlissingen*, on January 4, 1722, was followed two days later by the capture of the RAC ship *King Solomon*. Both ships were looted thoroughly before being burned. The *Flushing*, another Dutch ship, added to the haul.

By one means or another, alerts were being passed along the coast of Roberts's presence, and, sensing this, Roberts stood offshore out of sight of land as the flotilla tacked eastward, having already decided on the rich target that would be his next goal: the slave ship anchorage at Whydah, on the easternmost end of the Slave Coast.

Whydah was a sort of slaving "free port," where all slaving nations operated without hindrance. A Royal Africa Company fort was there, but was situated three miles inland and unable to supervise the anchorage and the long beach where wretched lines of slaves waited to be loaded into boats to be rowed out through the treacherous surf to the ships. The anchorage was the busiest on the coast, all transactions were done in gold; it was the sort of target Roberts could not resist. Notwithstanding the alarm that had undoubtedly been raised now along the Slave Coast to

Captain Bartho.Roberts *with two Ships, Viz the* Royal Fortune *and* Ranger, *takes
11 Sail in* Whydah *Road on the Coast of* Guiney, *January* 11ᵗʰ 172¼.

Roberts's ships, including the Royal Fortune, *flying both English colours and Roberts's
own distinctive ensigns, descend on the anchored slaving fleet using Roberts's methods
of intimidation through a display of noisy bravado and gunfire.*

his flotilla's presence, Roberts determined to act, with the same audacity
he had shown off Brazil and at Trepassey. Johnson relates what took place
on January 11, 1722:

> They came to *Whydah* with a St. *George's* Ensign, a black
> Silk Flag flying at their Mizen-Peek, and a Jack and Pendant
> of the same: The Flag had a Death in it, with an Hour-Glass
> in one Hand and cross Bones in the other, a Dart by it, and
> underneath a Heart dropping three Drops of Blood. —
> The Jack had a Man pourtray'd in it, with a flaming Sword
> in his Hand, and standing on two Skulls, subscribed *A B
> H* and *A M H i.e.* a *Barbadian's* and a *Martinican's* Head,
> as has been before taken Notice of. Here they found eleven

Sail in the Road, *English, French* and *Portuguese*; the *French* were three stout Ships of 30 Guns, and upwards of 100 Men each, yet when *Roberts* came to Fire, they, with the other Ships, immediately struck their Colours and surrendered to his Mercy. One Reason, it must be confess'd, of his easy Victory, was, the Commanders and a good part of the Men being ashore, according to the Custom of the Place, to receive the Cargoes, and return the Slaves, they being obliged to watch the Seasons for it, which otherwise, in so dangerous a Sea as here, would be impracticable. These all, except the *Porcupine*, ransomed with him for eight Pound of Gold-Dust, a Ship.[18]

The *Porcupine* was the scene of an appalling act of cruelty that hung forever over Roberts's reputation, but also provides a grim insight into the barbarity both of the age and the pirates themselves. The captain of the *Porcupine* would not agree to the ransoming arrangement, arguing he had no authority from the owners to do so. Exasperated, Roberts determined to burn the ship. *Porcupine*, however, had already been loaded with its cargo of slaves, so Roberts sent a longboat with orders to release the slaves and get them ashore, then burn the ship. But the boat's crew, "being in hast[e], and finding that unshackling them cost much Time and Labour, they actually set her on Fire, with eighty of those poor Wretches on Board, chained two and two together, under the miserable Choice of perishing by Fire or Water: Those who jumped overboard from the Flames were seized by Sharks ... and, in their Sight, tore Limb from Limb alive."[19]

With this horrid act of cruelty still hanging over the scene, Roberts received word from ashore that *Swallow* and *Weymouth* might be within just a few days' sail. Roberts met with his crews and persuaded them to put to sea instead of dissolving into the customary debauchery. He was said to have commented diplomatically, "Such brave fellows [as they were] cannot be supposed to be frightened at this News, yet that it were better to avoid dry Blows, which is the best that can be expected, if overtaken."[20] The crews agreed.

After having had a mere two days of degeneracy ashore, the pirate flotilla sailed, and by crew vote it was decided they would sail southwest for the island of Annobón, there to water and replenish and engage in their usual shore debauchery, for which they had an inexhaustible appetite. The plan, too, involved determining by vote their best next course. Many voices were already being raised calling for Brazil, a last grand capture, then a breakup of the crews afterward. But now fate interfered, for the winds went unexpectedly foul and the ships were forced closer to the mainland again before turning south, where they finally anchored in the lee of Cape Lopez, near the equator. There they would await the return of the steady winds that would carry them across the Atlantic to Brazil. It was a chance circumstance, but the vagaries of the wind had left Roberts open to his ultimate fate, and in the unravelling of that fate, as the ring of pursuit closed round him, it would be the wind that would deal him the final, deadly betrayal.

9

The Bloody End

As Roberts led his flotilla away from Whydah, a number of his men noted that one of the ransomed ships was a sleek and weatherly ex-privateer from Saint Malo. Ignoring the fact that Roberts had agreed to its ransom, these men took the privateer and brought it along, intending that it should be the new *Ranger*. But they were escaping an approaching threat, rather than leisurely departing into an ocean where no pursuit waited. As Sanders relates:

> As night fell on Saturday, 13 January 1722, the two pirate ships pulled away from Whydah, taking the French prize with them, leaving the *Porcupine* blazing in their wake. Captain Ogle arrived in HMS *Swallow* twenty-four hours later.
>
> Roberts had got away with it again. He had sailed into the very jaws of two of the most powerful British warships ever sent in pursuit of pirates, and yet had managed to pillage shipping along a 500-mile stretch of coast, leaving them twisting and turning in his wake, bewildered by the speed of his movement, and sailed away unharmed having taken a total of nineteen prizes. For all the simmering tensions within his own crew, he

must have felt invincible. There was even a bonus. As they pulled into open sea the pirates came across the *Whydah*, the small Royal Africa Company sloop which had escaped them two days before, enabling them to indulge once more their detestation of the company and its ships. They plundered it and [the pirates were] again given license to set it alight.[1]

There was irony in the fact that 1718, the year Roberts was taken into a life of piracy, in fact marked a turning point in the Crown's struggle to deal with the problem. Largely due to Roberts, piracy reached a high point from 1719 to 1721, and the Royal Navy's approach to the issue produced, at first, as Peter Earle comments, "no flood of successes, but there were some [successes] and the cumulative effect of these was sufficient to demonstrate to a wise pirate that the days of their 'very pleasant' way of life were numbered."[2]

The Royal Navy had begun to schedule and coordinate better the movements of single ships patrolling parts of the Atlantic, and as Earle points out, when the struggle began in earnest against the pirates of Roberts's era, Royal Navy ships were routinely undermanned, were permitted to buy stores only in Britain, and could not careen their ships while on station. But by 1722, ships were sailing with a full wartime complement of men; local supplies could be purchased after stores loaded in Britain were depleted; and careening was permitted wherever possible, eventually up to three times a year. These changes had vastly improved the navy's chances of catching pirates, and they lay behind the reality that Roberts was now being hunted by two powerful English warships that had chased him for eight months with the means and ability to destroy him.[3]

With their French prize, Roberts's ships made for the alternative shelter of Cape Lopez, south along the African coast. There, the conversion of the French prize began, but the surly restiveness of the crews again surfaced and led to renewed commitment that the next course for them all was to cross the Atlantic to the Brazil coast.[4]

The cracks were beginning to show indeed in the loose, voluntary organization and discipline of Roberts's crews, in part because of the ungovernable nature of the men, but also Roberts's increasing tendency to withdraw into himself and present what seemed to be an autocratic and unyielding attitude in many issues. It did not sit well with his mercurial shipmates. As Johnson relates,

[I]n the latter part of his Reign, he had run counter to [the leading men of his crew] in every Project that opposed his Opinion; for which, and because he grew reserved, and would not drink and roar at their Rate, a Cabal was formed to take away his Captainship, which Death did more effectually.[5]

As the ships lingered at anchor under Cape Lopez, Roberts had to contend with this increasing animosity among his men, and their proclivity to go ashore and submerge in "wenching" and drink made the most mundane maintenance tasks difficult. Sober and focused, the pirates were superb seamen; but too often their unconquerable thirst for brandy, rum, or other paralytic drink rendered them useless. In the aftermath of the final battle, it was observed, as Cordingly records, that

the trial of Bartholomew Roberts' crew at Cape Coast Castle reveals that many men spent most of their days incapacitated by drink. According to one witness, Robert Devins was never sober or fit for any duty, and Robert Johnson was so helplessly drunk that he had to be hoisted out of the ship with the aid of a block and tackle.[6]

Meanwhile, the pursuing warships *Swallow* and *Weymouth* had been slowly making their way eastward along the Gold and Slave Coasts, a tedious business of endless tacking, but accomplished so tardily that even with the terrible inroads that fever and other diseases were making in the naval crews, officials ashore wondered if Commodore Chaloner Ogle was hesitant to engage the well-armed and highly effective pirates. It took a final arrival at Whydah, barely hours after Roberts had sailed, for Ogle to suddenly gain new enthusiasm for the hunt, as ransomed shipowners there told them of Roberts's haul of gold, and on visiting the King of Whydah ashore, Ogle was promised personally fifty-six pounds of gold dust "if he should secure that rascal Roberts, who had long infested his coast."[7]

The dilemma now facing Ogle was to find out where Roberts had gone, and to do so with his ships in some semblance of fighting readiness. There was always the possibility that Roberts had steered for the open ocean, bound for the East Indies or Brazil — that thought was not unwelcome to Ogle, gold dust notwithstanding — but the likelihood was that the pirate flotilla was somewhere on the Lower Guinea coast, possibly as far south as Cape Lopez, or in the four-island chain. If Roberts had run westward, far offshore to avoid being sighted, and steered for Sierra Leone, the hunt was essentially lost; Ogle gambled it was not, and he steered for Prince's Island to careen his two ships, rest his crews, and restock his provisions. He sensed strongly that, somewhere to the east, Roberts lurked along the African coast and had not fled. In the event, he would be proven correct, and it was a fortunate decision.

With his ships refreshed, Ogle stood northeast into the Bight of Biafra, to see if any of the pestilential coves there held pirate ships careening. He then reversed his course and sailed back along the line of the four islands, to see either if the pirates had sheltered there or if there was word of their passing westward, which had been Roberts's hope. This proved fruitless, and Ogle decided on a sweep down the Lower Guinea coast as far as Cape Lopez. Crossing eastward again to the mainland, he made landfall at the mouth of the River Gabon on February 1, 1722. There he spoke to the crew of a Dutch ship that had run north past Cape Lopez, and asked if they had seen any suspicious vessels. The answer was a guarded no, but something in Ogle's mind clicked into place. As Richards relates,

> not paying too much attention to the information proffered, the *Swallow* left on the 3rd and searched the inlets towards the bay of Cape Lopez, the Cape itself lying 3 leagues, W.S.W. at daylight on the 5th. Hearing a gun firing at daybreak Captain Ogle pricked up his ears, and

focussing his eyes in the direction of the noise, saw three vessels at anchor under the Cape, and judged that they were pirates.[8]

Ogle's instincts had been correct: he had, at last, found his prey.

Ogle carefully considered his situation. He had two fifty-gun warships whose general appearance, if gun ports were closed and the correct ensigns flown, did not immediately reveal themselves to be warships, but possibly East Indiamen or other merchant vessels. His firepower was overwhelming, but he had two important limitations: as large, square-rigged vessels, both *Swallow* and *Weymouth* would work to windward with slow difficulty, and it was unlikely the ships could match the hull speeds of the somewhat handier pirate vessels, particularly if they had been careened and had clean bottoms. In addition, the pirates were expert seamen — when sober — when they had to be, as mentioned. Both Royal Navy vessels had been forced to take aboard new crewmen from the African slaving ports after losing large numbers of men to fever shortly after arriving on the African coast: from July 28 to September 20, 1721, the ships "buried 100 Men in three Weeks Time, and reduced the Remainder of the Ships Companies into so sickly a State, that it was with Difficulty they brought them to sail."[9]

To get at the pirates, therefore, Ogle had either to work his ships painfully by a zigzag course of shallow tacks up to get (hopefully) to windward of his quarry, or induce them to raise anchors and run down to close with him. His guns could fire almost a ton of metal round shot up to three miles, but ship motion and powder inconsistencies meant successful actions had to be fought at closer ranges: Ogle needed to close to almost point-blank range if he was to have any hope at all of defeating the pirate ships.

Weymouth, at this point, was almost out of sight back along the coast northward, while *Swallow* had managed to work well, by long, tedious tacking, up into the great lee formed by Cape Lopez, where the three pirate vessels rode at anchor, sheltered from the prevailing wind and swell out of the south or southeast. *Swallow*'s paint scheme and rig did not immediately identify it as a warship, and Ogle may have hoisted false

In command of the Royal Navy frigate Swallow, *accompanied by the frigate* Weymouth, Chaloner Ogle *managed by virtue of determination and a perceptive understanding of Roberts's movements on the West African coast to bring him to battle off Cape Lopez, where foul weather and effective naval gunnery allowed him to bring an end to the pirate's career.*

colours at this point, as the pirate lookouts on the anchored flotilla identified *Swallow* as a Portuguese merchantman. The pirates were for having at it, so Roberts is said to have remarked, "There is sugar in the offing, have it brought in so that we have no more mumbling." Sugar was an important ingredient in a favourite crew drink known as punch. Accordingly, the new French vessel of thirty-two guns, the new *Ranger*, halted preparations to careen ashore, restored her rig, and was rapidly manned by volunteers from all three ships. Under the command of one of Roberts's lieutenants, James Skyrm, the *Ranger* lifted its anchor, fell off the wind, and crowded on sail to run down ahead of the wind toward *Swallow*.

Ogle had approached a dangerous shoal as he tacked back and forth across the bay, downwind from the pirate anchorage. This forced him to turn or "wear," which had falsely convinced Skyrm that *Swallow* was fleeing, as a merchantman might. As Ogle related in his official report:

> On the 5th of February at daylight, I saw Cape Lopez bearing W.S.W. about three leagues [nine miles]; and at the same time discovered three ships at anchor under the Cape, which I believed to be the Pyrates, two of them having pendants flying. I was obliged to haul off N.W. and W.N.W. to clear the Frenchman's Bank, the wind at S.S.E. and in less than an hour one of the three got under sail and gave me chase; and I to give her fair opportunity of coming up with me without being discovered, kept on the same course, with the same sail aboard I had when I first saw her.[10]

Ogle deliberately allowed *Swallow* to simulate "bad steerage, so that her rate of head way would not leave her pursuer far in the rear." By half-past ten both ships were well out of sight to the northward, and Ogle shortened sail to allow the *Ranger* to come up. The surprise for Skyrm was not long in being revealed, as Johnson recounts:

> The Pyrates now drew nigh enough to fire their Chase Guns; they hoisted the black Flag that was worn in

Whydah Road, and got their Spritsail Yard along-ships, with Intent to board; no one having ever asked, all this while, what Country Sh'p they took the Chase to be; they would have her to be a *Portuguese*, (Sugar being then a Commodity among them,) and were swearing every Minute at the Wind or Sails to expedite so sweet a Chase; but, alas, all turned sour in an Instant: It was with the utmost Consternation they saw her suddenly bring to, and hawl up her lower Ports, now within Pistol-shot, and struck their black Flag upon it directly. After the first Surprize was over, they kept firing at a Distance, hoisted it again, and vapoured with their Cutlashes on the Poop; tho' wisely endeavouring at the same Time to get away. Being now at their Wits end, boarding was proposed by the Heads of them, and so to make one desperate Push; but the Motion not being well seconded, and their Main-Top-Mast coming down by a Shot, after two Hours firing, it was declin'd; they grew Sick, struck their Colours, and called out for Quarters; having had 10 Men killed out right, and 20 wounded, without the loss or hurt of one of the King's Men. She had 32 Guns, mann'd with 16 *French* Men, 20 Negroes, and 77 *English*. The Colours were thrown over board, that they might not rise in Judgment, nor be display'd in Tryumph over them.[11]

That the pirates had initially surrendered, but then resumed the fight was remarkable given that their thirty-two guns were opposed by *Swallow*'s fifty. They knew their fate if captured, and desperation may have played a role. Ogle fought the engagement well, directing his fire to bring down *Ranger*'s rigging and inflict casualties on deck, but not seriously to damage the valuable prize of the hull: rigging could be repaired. There were no casualties on the warship, but twenty-six of Skyrm's men were killed or wounded, he himself losing a leg in the cannonade. As *Swallow*'s prize crew rowed over by longboat to take possession of *Ranger*, a huge flash and billow of smoke from aft in the pirate ship announced a failed attempt by six of the pirates to blow up the ship. They had fired a pistol into the remaining powder in the magazine. Although Ogle considered setting *Ranger* on fire, he determined instead to repair it, and led it off with a jury-rig, prize crew, and the pirates below in shackles to Prince's Island. On seeing *Ranger* safely at anchor there, Ogle took three days to return to the vicinity of Cape Lopez, arriving there February 9, 1722. To his surprise, there were again *three* ships at anchor under the Cape's shelter, clarified when it was evident "through the glass" that one was a new prize, just taken by the pirates. Ogle realized that the pirates had no idea of *Ranger*'s defeat and that a drunken celebration had likely followed the capture of the new ship. If he could tack up into gun range of the anchored flotilla, no better chance would be available to end Roberts's career.

The sky had become ominous, with dark, scudding cloud low over-head, flashes of lightning in the distance, and occasional curtains of grey obscuring rain moving across the gunmetal surface of the sea. As *Royal Fortune*'s few lookouts blearily perceived the dark, ominous shape of a heavy ship punching its way up toward them with the taut efficiency of a warship, Roberts was entertaining the young captain of his recent capture, a ten-gun "pink" named *Neptune*, to breakfast in his cabin, while *Swallow*'s crew were already beginning to sink into their usual post-capture revelling that would lead inevitably to paralytic drinking. The mumbled warnings of the lookouts produced little alarm; rather, as Richards relates,

> The arch-pirate was so engrossed in a discourse with his young captive that he at first ignored the report about the approach of a strange ship: neither were his men wor-ried about such a commonplace occurrence but merely discussed with each other whether she was a Portuguese trader, a French slaver or the returning *Ranger*. They had already divided their forces but it never occurred to them to provide for the possibility of the *Ranger* being defeated, an event that would prove a source of danger to them. Instead of being on their alert, they debated

merrily, after their carousal aboard the new prize, as to what kind of reception they would give the stranger, and whether to salute her or not. In those days it was not easy to distinguish a warship from a merchantman, for the latter sometimes flew the prohibited red ensign and carried guns; furthermore, neither officers nor men in the Navy had by then adopted uniforms.[12]

Roberts arrived on deck, peering off to leeward through the rain and mist at the dark shape of the approaching ship. Suddenly it was coldly clear to him that this was not the returning *Ranger*, a fact confirmed when one pirate who had sailed in *Swallow* came up to Roberts in some agitation and identified it. Roberts knew at that moment he was in for a serious fight, and he quickly gave orders for the crew of the *Little Ranger* to cross to *Royal Fortune* before the dark ship closed, which was confusing the issue by flying French colours. From the former *Swallow* man, Roberts learned the warship sailed well on a reach, across the wind, but not well on a run before it. If *Royal Fortune* was to escape *Swallow*'s fifty guns, it would have to get past it and run northward ahead of the wind, showing its heels.

Rain lashed the deck and lightning was now flashing intermittently overhead, with cracking peals of thunder. It was an apocalyptic setting, and Roberts seemed to know it, for suddenly he appeared back on deck resplendent in a suit of scarlet velvet, a red feather in his hat, gold chains and a crucifix around his neck, and slung about with two brace of pistols on silken lanyards. Briskly he barked orders over the wind's howl and sea noise to get the ship underway, and the drink-addled, hungover men groped their way to their stations through the dark, driving rain.

As the full force of the tropical storm swept over the scene, *Swallow* was looming up toward *Royal Fortune*, spray wreathing its bows as it punched through the dark swells. Now from aloft and the ship's stern staff, British ensigns and jacks streamed out, and a lance-like commissioning pennant rose to the mainmast head. As *Swallow* cut its cable and fell off the wind, Roberts replied with ironic British colours and his own dramatic black ensign. He stood on his quarterdeck by the helm, drenched now in the heavy rain, his mind fixed on his plan of escape:

Royal Fortune would let drop and sheet home all sail, and drive ahead of the wind directly for *Swallow*. Roberts would accept the risk of a single broadside from the warship at close range in the hopes that the speed of *Royal Fortune*'s passing, the blinding rain, and the wind would limit the British gunnery's effectiveness, and *Royal Fortune* could rush past and escape northward to the open sea, faster than *Swallow* could follow.

At first, the plan seemed to be working. With his groggy crew crouching wide-eyed by the guns or gripping the sail-handling lines, at 11:00 a.m. that fateful morning *Royal Fortune* rushed in close along *Swallow*'s flank. The wind held, with tremendous blasts of lightning and thunder overhead now garishly illuminating the scene. As *Swallow* came abeam, Roberts barked out the order to fire, and a ragged broadside flamed out from *Royal Fortune*'s side. The open sea lay ahead; *Royal Fortune* surged on, wreathed in her own gun smoke. But then, in the next instant, a tremendous broadside licked out in twenty-foot flames from *Swallow*'s side, and *Royal Fortune* shook from the concussions. Rushing out of the smoke of *Swallow*'s broadside, it seemed for a moment that *Royal Fortune* was free: Roberts's gamble had paid off. But now the wind played its fateful role: *Royal Fortune* entered a sudden calm and her canvas went slack, the ship still within range of the warship's guns. As *Royal Fortune* wallowed down, losing headway, Ogle was able to fall off the wind and present his broadside again to the pirate. Another rippling broadside punched out again from the *Swallow*, and *Royal Fortune* shuddered under the impact of the second course of flying round shot.

On *Royal Fortune*'s deck, dazed men rushed to where Roberts had stood, cursing him for not giving new orders, only to see his scarlet-clad body slumped over a gun carriage. He was drenched in blood: his throat had been ripped open by flying splinters or grapeshot, and Bartholomew Roberts, king of the Atlantic pirates, was dead. In tears, the men who found him wrapped his body with a heavy chain and thrust it out through a gun port, and he sank away in his scarlet velvet into the sea he had commanded for a few short years.

Leaderless, the pirates fought on, but the cause was hopeless now, and it was only a matter of time before *Swallow*'s guns wreaked irreparable destruction on the stricken *Royal Fortune*. As Sanders recounts,

Just for a moment it looked as if Roberts might have got away with it. But then the crew's night of revelry took its toll. One man simply passed out on the deck having fired his gun. Many others were little better and the pirates' steering was erratic. By now the storm was gaining in strength. One clap of thunder "seemed like the rattling of 10,000 small arms within three yards of our heads" [one man] later recalled, and the simultaneous bolt of lightning split the top of HMS *Swallow*'s main-mast. But, with the wind swirling around unpredictably, the warship was soon gaining ground once more on the *Royal Fortune*. At half past one, it came close enough to deliver another broadside. As the smoke cleared, the men on HMS *Swallow* saw the pirate's main-mast come crashing down. Shortly afterwards the pirates signalled surrender.[13]

The career of the acknowledged king of the Atlantic pirates, whose success had begun with the dramatic transformation into power during a summer spent in what would become Canadian waters, had ended, perhaps fittingly, in a storm-riven, bloody climax off a faraway African coast. His black flag would fly no more.

The aftermath of Roberts's defeat was predictable. With their various prizes in tow, *Swallow* rejoined *Weymouth* and carried north the surviving pirates — 268 men, of which 77 were Africans and 187 Europeans. These would have included seamen and captives recently taken in ships captured by Roberts.

The men were brought to the forbidding battlements of Cape Coast Castle, where on March 28, 1722, a Vice-Admiralty court was convened. The court determined to consider each man individually, and, as David Cordingly relates, "apart from nineteen men who died of their wounds before the trial, all the white men taken by HMS *Swallow* were examined by the court.... Within three weeks of the formal opening of the proceedings, fifty-two men had been hanged, twenty had been condemned to penal servitude in Africa, and seventeen had been sentenced to imprisonment in London's Marshalsea Prison."[14]

Charles Johnson's 1724 account of Roberts's career provides a detailed record of the proceedings of the court, which made every effort, it appeared, to acquit those who clearly were present due to captivity or could convince the court they had been forced into servitude with the pirates. In any event, seventy-four prisoners were acquitted and two more were "respited," which meant their cases were unclear and were referred to "His Majesty's Pleasure." One of those men died, but the second received a King's Pardon on returning to England.[15]

The condemned men, having been found to be "Traitors, Robbers, Pyrates and Common Enemies of Mankind," were put to death in group executions through the month of April 1722. Cordingly observes the particular nature of the sentences at the Marshalsea Prison:

> Imprisonment in the Marshalsea was reserved for those who were so constantly drunk that they were not fit for duty; for "a half-witted fellow … ever in some monkey-like foolish action," and for a prisoner like Elizabeth Trengrove, a passenger in the *Swallow*, of being "very rude, swearing and cursing and forcing her hooped petticoat off."[16]

The men sentenced to penal servitude in Africa would all die within months. For those condemned to execution on the spot, the sentence of the president of the court was stated in unequivocal language:

> Ye, and each of you, are adjudged and sentenced, to be carried back to the Place from whence ye came, from thence to the Place of Execution, without the Gates of this Castle, and there within the Flood-Marks, to be hanged by the Neck till ye are dead. After this ye, and each of you shall be taken down, and your Bodies hanged in Chains.[17]

To be hanged in the eighteenth century certainly provided Roberts's "sower look or two at Choaking," as the prisoner was suspended, hands tied, from a bar overhead by a noose around the neck, which killed them by slow strangulation as they swung and struggled. At the moment of that death, some of the prisoners may well have wished that the ships' powder magazines could have been touched off and the lot "blown merrily to Hell together."

As they were brought out of the gloom of the cells and led in the searing heat to their deaths, some of the pirates expressed repentance, and even called out to observers not to repeat their mistakes; but foremost among them was a hardened disdain for the court and its charges, having "exclaimed against the Severity of the Court, … [they] were so harden'd, as to curse, and wish the same Justice might overtake all the Members of it, as had been dealt to them. *They were poor Rogues,* they said, *and so hang'd, while others, no less guilty in another Way, escaped.*"[18]

For Chaloner Ogle, his success over Roberts not only brought to a close a chapter in the history of Atlantic piracy, but led to his own profit and advancement. Once the trial at Cape Coast Castle was over, Ogle shepherded his three pirate prizes and *Swallow* across the Atlantic to the West Indies. He paused at Barbados to sell some of the prize goods in the ships, and then carried on to Port Royal, Jamaica, for sale of the remainder and of the prize vessels themselves. The flotilla arrived off Port Royal on August 14, 1722, and the off-loading of the pirate vessels began oddly, with barrels of water being taken off first, Port Royal having no source of fresh water.

Load after load of prize goods from *Royal Fortune* and the other ships were brought ashore — but then fate in the form of foul weather intervened again. On August 28, 1722, before the off-loading of the pirate vessels was complete, a hurricane struck Port Royal with terrifying force at half-past eight in the morning. Chaloner Ogle, at anchor in *Swallow* off Port Royal, later wrote that there was "as much wind in my opinion as could possibly blow out of the heavens … all the merchantmen in the harbour foundered or drove ashore excepting one sloop."

The surgeon of the *Swallow*, John Atkins, observed in a later account that only six of the fifty ships in harbour survived the storm, although dismasted. The official list was seventy-three vessels, of which fifty were lost. Eleven survived at anchor, two more were beached ashore, and ten of the wrecked ships could be salvaged later. The *Royal Fortune* and *Little Ranger* were driven across the harbour and smashed to bits on Saltpond Hill Rocks, while the French-built *Ranger* Skyrm had commanded survived, although heavily damaged.

Atkins gives a vivid picture of the storm's effect:

> Within it was worse, for the waters sapping the foundations, gave continual and just apprehensions of the houses falling, as in effect half of them did, and buried their inhabitants.... Wrecks, and drowned men were everywhere seen along the shore, general complaints of loss at land which made it a melancholy scene, and to finish the misfortune, the slackness of the sea breezes, calms, and lightning, stagnating waters, broods of insects thence, and a shock or two of earthquake that succeeded to the hurricane, combined to spread a baneful influence, and brought on a contagious distemper, fatal for some months through the island.[19]

Chaloner Ogle managed to sell the *Ranger* to a buyer in Port Royal for over five thousand pounds, but did not share any of those riches with his crews.[20]

Ogle's success against Roberts led to further honours and, in 1725, payment of the prize money to him and his crews. On returning to England, he was knighted by George I in May of 1723 for his success in ridding the seas of Roberts, the first knighthood to be awarded for anti-piracy action. He went on to have a colourful and lucrative career, notably in the War of 1739–48, became a member of Parliament, and died at home in 1750 with the rank of admiral of the fleet. His greatest career success would remain the long-ago battle off a storm-swept African cape that arguably brought about the beginning of the end of the "Golden Age of Piracy."

Ogle would slowly vanish from memory and the public mind; but not so the odd, violent, lost men whom he pursued, who remain a source of fascination to the present day. Roberts's ships were torn to pieces in the environment he had died in, surrounded by the roar and fury of a violent storm. It was oddly appropriate that there was no calm to their passing.

10

The Lasting Myth

The defeat of Roberts's flotilla and his own death, for many historians, marks the end of the most significant era of Western piracy, or at least the beginning of its decline. Ogle's action in 1722 was followed by other captures and executions in 1723 and 1724, so that by 1726 very few pirates remained in comparison to the numbers that had once choked Atlantic trade almost to a standstill. Naval pursuit had become more and more proficient; colonial governors saw less value in clandestine dealing with pirates than in effective support of their merchants and their trade; and the law had been strengthened against any form of co-operation or collaboration with pirate crews. As Peter Earle observes:

> [A]t last the golden age of piracy came to an end. The freedom- and drink-loving pirates had their moment of fame, but in the long run the navy, the law and the self-destructive nature of the pirates themselves ensured that piracy was not an occupation with a very long life expectancy.[1]

The reputation of pirates as fearsome sea warriors who would fight to the death, as Blackbeard had done, and with whom the navy was once loath to close, was shattered by the fact that two heavily armed and fully crewed pirate vessels were taken without the death of a single Royal Navy man or officer. Earle points out the pirate/prisoner William Snelgrave was not surprised at the one-sided loss, as he felt the pirates "were so much in drink, that there could have been no order or conduct amongst them in an engagement."

John Atkins of the *Swallow* had the most effective word on the matter:

> Discipline is an excellent path to victory, and courage, like a trade, is gained by an apprenticeship, when strictly kept up to rules and exercise. The pirates, though singly fellows of courage, yet wanting such a tie of order and some director to unite that force, were a contemptible enemy. They neither killed nor wounded a man in the taking; which ever must be the fate of such rabble.[2]

Atkins overlooked the fact that perhaps Roberts's death was decisive in the victory, for even allowing Atkins's model of the pirates as an undisciplined rabble, Roberts had managed, within a social order established by the authority-averse pirates, to achieve some stunning victories through audacity and cunning. But the image of the pirate vessel as a fearsome and indefatigable terror of the seas had been irrevocably shattered.

Piracy in the sailing ship era would never be fully eradicated, but after the climax of the 1720s, the pirate as an ominous and feared threat on the horizon of oceanic trade gradually faded in both the official and public mind, until finally, in the late nineteenth century, *The Pirates of Penzance*, the British comic light opera by Gilbert and Sullivan, was able to portray a pirate band as a group of essentially nice fellows of good breeding who had simply gone wrong. Fiction, and, much later, film, came to romanticize the figure of the pirate into a character representing freedom, adventure, and a kind of forgivable roguery. The reality, of course, had been quite the opposite. As David Cordingly succinctly puts it,

> [Pirates] were tough and ruthless men capable of savage cruelty and murder.... Most pirates were by nature rebellious and lazy. They were notorious for foul language,

and for prolonged bouts of drinking, which frequently led to quarrels and violence. They came together in an uneasy partnership, attracted by the lure of plunder and the desire for an easy life.[3]

Piracy, as Rediker explains somewhat more gently, "was a way of life voluntarily chosen, for the most part, by large numbers of men who directly challenged the ways of the society from which they excepted themselves."[4]

In the way of life they chose, however, the pirates also laid the certainty of their own destruction, of which they were very likely aware. Their indiscipline and the short-term pursuit of nihilistic pleasure and gratification displayed, one might argue, an unspoken awareness that they were dead men to begin with. The vastly unfair society that put riches or privilege forever out of their reach would turn on them once they undid the bonds of law-abiding servitude and reached for those treasures. Most knew this, and, rather than attempting, as very few pirates did, to keep some of their plunder and aspire to a quiet life ashore, most, as Cordingly grimly confirms, "preferred to spend their plunder in an orgy of drinking, gambling and whoring when they returned to port."[5] A short life, and a merry one, was to be their lot, they knew. And for most, it was.

Hidden in the pirate lifestyle, however, were strictures as binding as any unfair laws of commerce or work at sea, for the pirates' hatred of perceived betterment and personal privilege led them to be as ruthless in limiting personal freedom among themselves as any hardbitten naval boatswain. The romantic view of Atlantic pirates of the sailing ship era seems to continue, even as modern pirates brandishing assault rifles rather than flintlocks or cutlasses reveal that piracy was then and is now a brutal, criminal process that has far less adventure and personal liberation in it than is usually portrayed. To the persistent student of history, the figure of the European Atlantic pirates that is eventually revealed is of doomed individuals deserving of an odd kind of pity at the waste of their lives, leavened with repulsion at the cruelty, destruction, and criminality of their behaviour. Perhaps, as in the line from the old song, they were "more to be pitied than censured"; but for the most part they were rarely deserving of anything beyond revulsion. Romance does not belong with their story.

The figure of Bartholomew Roberts remains shadowy and indistinct, as we have only his observed behaviour to draw from in creating an image of him: except for one or two letters, he left no writings that would reveal a deeper character. Tall, darkly handsome, physically strong and courageous, quick to temper, obviously gifted with an almost Nelsonian audacity and tactical sense, he managed to lead with fatalism and abandon crews of desperate men whose abandonment of lawfulness he seems to have shared easily, for unknown reasons. A solitary figure, abstemious in personal habits, oddly religious, drawn neither to women nor to men for intimacy, he was capable of surprising warmth to prisoners and reputedly more protective of women than was common among pirates. Roberts exhibited many of the characteristics of broad vision and self-restraint that marked many other men tasked with leadership at sea; had Roberts not embraced a hopeless criminality, and been powered by more constructive urges into a merchant shipping or naval career, his astonishing gifts of leadership in a more disciplined setting might have seen him with achievements on the order of Drake, Hawkins, Benbow, or later Cook and even Nelson. The seeds of greatness were there within him — four hundred or more plundered ships on the Atlantic marked some unique gifts — but circumstance and perhaps personal character, or a hidden, bitter disappointment — even heartbreak — from the past prevented their flowering. At a key moment in his life he was presented figuratively with a door marked *Doom*, and with a shrug, he went through it. He would be remembered as the "Dread Pirate Roberts" and the uncrowned king of the Atlantic pirate world, but the impoverished Welsh farmboy might have achieved something in history far more honourable.

It was in the waters of what would eventually be Canada that Roberts was transformed from a minor criminal into a dominant, fighting commodore. For several key months over the summer of 1721, with his raids at Canso, off Louisbourg, at Ferryland, and most tellingly at Trepassey, Roberts's audacity and ruthless courage led him through ship capture and plunder to go from being a defeated, small-time pirate to the master of a powerful equivalent to a warship, leading a growing flotilla that would bring West Indian trade to a fearful halt. When he sailed south out of Canadian waters, his new black ensigns at the masthead and stern staff, he was the dominant pirate of the Atlantic trading world. Like a man otherwise as unlike him as it was possible to be, the diligent Yorkshireman James Cook a half-century later, Roberts found the tools of his destiny in Canadian waters. The place does have that effect on people.

Notes

Chapter 1: Drawn to the Sea

1. Aubrey Burl, *Black Barty: The Real Pirate of the Caribbean* (Gloucestershire: Sutton, 2006), 55.
2. Richard Sanders, *If a Pirate I Must Be ...: The True Story of Bartholomew Roberts, King of the Caribbean* (London: Aurum Press, 2007), 17.
3. Reginald J.W. Hammond, ed., *The Complete Wales: A Survey of the Main Holiday Areas and Places of Interest* (London: Ward Lock, 1972), 14.
4. George Owen, cited in Saunders, *If a Pirate I Must Be ...*, 16.
5. Colin Woodard, *The Republic of Pirates: Being the True and Surprising Story of the Caribbean Pirates and the Man Who Brought Them Down* (New York: Harcourt, 2007), 320.
6. Marcus Rediker, *The Slave Ship: A Human History* (New York: Penguin, 2007), 227.
7. Victor Suthren, *To Go Upon Discovery: James Cook and Canada* (Toronto: Dundurn Press, 2000), 21–28 passim.
8. Marcus Rediker, *Villains of All Nations: Atlantic Pirates in the Golden Age* (Boston: Beacon Press, 2004), 57.
9. Ibid., 57–58.
10. Ibid., 59.

11. Stanley Richards, *Black Bart* (Llandybie, Wales: Christopher Davies, 1966), 20.

Chapter 2: A Dark Enterprise

1. Herbert S. Klein, *The Atlantic Slave Trade*, 2nd ed. (New York: Cambridge University Press, 2010), 75.
2. Ibid., 8–9.
3. Rediker, *The Slave Ship*, 42.
4. Ibid., 46.
5. Ibid., 5.
6. Ibid., 6.
7. Hugh Thomas, *The Slave Trade: The Story of the Atlantic Slave Trade: 1440–1870* (New York: Touchstone, 1997), 243.
8. Klein, *The Atlantic Slave Trade*, 39.
9. Thomas, *The Slave Trade*, 230–31.
10. Rediker, *The Slave Ship*, 85.
11. Thomas, *The Slave Trade*, 237.
12. Rediker, *The Slave Ship*, 351.
13. Ibid., 150.
14. Ibid., 227.
15. James Field Stanfield, quoted in Rediker, *The Slave Ship*, 139.
16. Ibid., 239.
17. Ibid., 217.
18. Klein, *The Atlantic Slave Trade*, 146.
19. Rediker, *The Slave Ship*, 45.

Chapter 3: The Sweet Trade

1. Dan Conlin, *Pirates of the Atlantic: Robbery, Murder and Mayhem Off the Canadian East Coast* (Halifax: Formac, 2009), 8.
2. Peter Earle, *The Pirate Wars* (New York: St. Martin's Griffin, 2003), 146.
3. Ibid., 149.
4. David Cordingly, *Life Among the Pirates: The Romance and the Reality* (London: Little, Brown, 1995), 224.

5. Rediker, *The Slave Ship*, 187–221 passim.
6. Conlin, *Pirates of the Atlantic*, 22.
7. Rediker, *Villains of All Nations*, 143.
8. Douglas Botting, *The Pirates* (New York: Time-Life Books, 1978), 25.
9. Conlin, *Pirates of the Atlantic*, 7.
10. Cordingly, *Life Among the Pirates*, 83.
11. Marcus Rediker, *Outlaws of the Atlantic: Sailors, Pirates, and Motley Crews in the Age of Sail* (Boston: Beacon, 2014), 50.
12. Ibid., 67
13. Earle, *The Pirate Wars*, 26.
14. Ibid., 159.
15. Richards, *Black Bart*, 17.
16. Cordingly, *Life Among the Pirates*, 21.
17. Earle, *The Pirate Wars*, 166–67.
18. Vice-Admiral Edward Vernon, quoted in John Hely Owen, *War at Sea Under Queen Anne, 1702–1708* (New York: Cambridge University Press, 1938), 25.
19. Cordingly, *Life Among the Pirates*, 22.
20. Rediker, *Villains of All Nations*, 9.
21. Earle, *The Pirate Wars*, 25.
22. David Cordingly, *Seafaring Women: Adventures of Pirate Queens, Female Stowaways, and Sailors' Wives* (New York: Random House, 2001), 146.
23. Cordingly, *Life Among the Pirates*, 114.
24. Earle, *The Pirate Wars*, 168.
25. Ibid., 163.
26. William Gilkerson, *Boarders Away: With Steel-Edged Weapons and Polearms* (Lincoln, RI: Andrew Mobray, 1991), 23.
27. Cordingly, *Life Among the Pirates*, 111.
28. Botting, *The Pirates*, 47.
29. Rediker, *Villains of All Nations*, 16.
30. Charles Johnson, *A General History of the Pyrates, from Their First Rise and Settlement in the Island of Providence, the Present Time*, 2nd ed. (London: T. Warner, 1724), 230–32.
31. Earle, *The Pirate Wars*, 11.

32. Ibid., 12.
33. Samuel Johnson, quoted in Rediker, *Outlaws of the Atlantic*, 65.

Chapter 4: Piracy and Canada

1. Conlin, *Pirates of the Atlantic*, 12.
2. Victor Suthren, *The Island of Canada: How Three Oceans Shaped Our Nation* (Toronto: Thomas Allen, 2009), 133–48 passim.
3. Conlin, *Pirates of the Atlantic*, 9–11.
4. Ibid., 16.

Chapter 5: The Blade Unsheathed

1. Rediker, *Villains of All Nations*, 23.
2. Angus Konstam, *The Pirate Ship 1660–1730* (Oxford: Osprey, 2003), 230.
3. Earle, *The Pirate Wars*, 165.
4. Burl, *Black Barty*, 47.
5. David Cordingly, *Under the Black Flag: The Romance and the Reality of Life Among the Pirates* (New York: Harcourt, Brace, 1996), 108.
6. Konstam, *The Pirate Ship*, 231.
7. Rediker, *Outlaws*, 78.
8. Konstam, *The Pirate Ship*, 231.
9. Johnson, *A General History of the Pyrates*, 186.
10. Konstam, *The Pirate Ship*, 231.
11. Botting, *The Pirates*, 159.
12. Johnson, *A General History of the Pyrates*, 187.
13. Burl, *Black Barty*, 51.
14. Sanders, *If a Pirate I Must Be …*, 32.
15. Johnson, *A General History of the Pyrates*, 272–73.
16. Richards, *Black Bart*, 22.
17. Ibid., 22.
18. Ibid., 25.
19. Johnson, *A General History of the Pyrates*, 206.
20. Ibid., 206.
21. Richards, *Black Bart*, 25.

22. Johnson, *A General History of the Pyrates*, 207.
23. Richards, *Black Bart*, 25.
24. Johnson, *A General History of the Pyrates*, 210.
25. Ibid., 209.
26. Ibid.
27. Ibid., 210.

Chapter 6: Armed to the Teeth

1. Richards, *Black Bart*, 29.
2. Johnson, *A General History of the Pyrates*, 211.
3. Cordingly, *Life Among the Pirates*, 102.
4. Richards, *Black Bart*, 30.
5. Ibid., 31.
6. Donald G. Shomette, *Pirates on the Chesapeake: Being a True History of Pirates, Picaroons, and Raiders on Chesapeake Bay, 1610–1807* (Centreville, MD: Tidewater, 1985), 218.
7. Ibid., 218.
8. Johnson, *A General History of the Pyrates*, 223–24.
9. Ibid., 226–27.
10. Rediker, *Villains of All Nations*, 154–55.
11. Ibid., 131.
12. Richards, *Black Bart*, 33.
13. Johnson, *A General History of the Pyrates*, 233.
14. Richards, *Black Bart*, 39.
15. Ibid., 39.
16. Johnson, *A General History of the Pyrates*, 215.
17. Ibid., 216.
18. Earle, *The Pirate Wars*, 33.
19. Conlin, *Pirates of the Atlantic*, 28.
20. Ibid., 5.
21. Ibid., 29.
22. Johnson, *A General History of the Pyrates*, 237–38.
23. Conlin, *Pirates of the Atlantic*, 30.
24. Johnson, *A General History of the Pyrates*, 238–39.

Chapter 7: A Grim Vengeance

1. Johnson, *A General History of the Pyrates*, 239–40.
2. Rediker, *Villains of All Nations*, 86–87.
3. Johnson, *A General History of the Pyrates*, 241–42.
4. Richards, *Black Bart*, 48.
5. Ibid., 49.
6. Johnson, *A General History of the Pyrates*, 240.
7. Cordingly, *Life Among the Pirates*, 154.
8. Richards, *Black Bart*, 52.
9. Shomette, *Pirates on the Chesapeake*, 228.
10. Richards, *Black Bart*, 59.

Chapter 8: Plunder and Loot

1. Earle, *The Pirate Wars*, 139.
2. Shomette, *Pirates on the Chesapeake*, 238.
3. Rediker, *Villains of All Nations*, 29.
4. Earle, *The Pirate Wars*, 150.
5. Rediker, *Villains of All Nations*, 15–16.
6. Cordingly, *Life Among the Pirates*, 196.
7. Rediker, *Villains of All Nations*, 27.
8. Richards, *Black Bart*, 60.
9. Chad M. Gulseth, "Black Bart's *Ranger*," in *Pieces of Eight: More Archaeology of Piracy*, ed. Charles R. Ewen and Russell K. Skowronek (Tallahassee: University Press of Florida, 2016), 95.
10. Richards, *Black Bart*, 63.
11. Rediker, *Outlaws of the Atlantic*, 80–81, apparently quoting William Smith, *A New Voyage to Guinea*, 2nd ed. (London: John Nourse, 1745), 42. Online at http://bit.ly/2GojQzP.
12. Richards, *Black Bart*, 63.
13. Rediker, *The Slave Ship*, 22.
14. Johnson, *A General History of the Pyrates*, 255.
15. Rediker, *Villains of All Nations*, 48.
16. Richards, *Black Bart*, 68.

17. Ibid., 69.
18. Johnson, *A General History of the Pyrates*, 259–60.
19. Ibid., 261.
20. Ibid.

Chapter 9: The Bloody End

1. Sanders, *If a Pirate I Must Be …*, 211–12.
2. Earle, *The Pirate Wars*, 192.
3. Ibid., 186.
4. Richards, *Black Bart*, 27.
5. Johnson, *A General History of the Pyrates*, 214.
6. Cordingly, *Life Among the Pirates*, 114.
7. The source of this quote I have been unable to confirm, but have included it as it seems very much in character of the times, and plausible. Rediker has it in *The Slave Ship*, and it also appears in, for example, Robert Norris, "A Journey to the Court of Bossa Ahadee," *Colonial Journal* 1, no. 2 (July 1816): 323; which is quoted in *The Terrific Register* 2 (1825): 531.
8. Richards, *Black Bart*, 82.
9. Johnson, *A General History of the Pyrates*, 262.
10. Admiralty records 1/2242, Public Record Office, cited in Gulseth, "Black Bart's *Ranger*," 97–99.
11. Johnson, *A General History of the Pyrates*, 267.
12. Richards, *Black Bart*, 87.
13. Sanders, *If a Pirate I Must Be …*, 220.
14. Cordingly, *Under the Black Flag*, 230.
15. Johnson, *A General History of the Pyrates*, 326.
16. Cordingly, *Under the Black Flag*, 233.
17. Johnson, *A General History of the Pyrates*, 298.
18. Ibid., 286.
19. J. Atkins, *A Full and Exact Account, of the Tryal of All the Pirates, Lately Taken by Captain Ogle On Board the Swallow Man Of War, on the Coast of Guinea* (Warwick: J. Roberts, 1723), 47.
20. Gulseth, "Black Bart's *Ranger*," 100.

Chapter 10: The Lasting Myth

1. Earle, *The Pirate Wars*, 206.
2. Atkins, quoted in Earle, *The Pirate Wars*, 198.
3. Cordingly, *Life Among the Pirates*, 23.
4. Rediker, *Outlaws of All Nations*, 64.
5. Cordingly, *Life Among the Pirates*, 209.

Selected Bibliography

The following few works allow Bartholomew Roberts's career to be best understood within the larger picture of European piracy in the early eighteenth century. For the most scholarly and detailed examination of Roberts's transformative Trepassey raid, see Olaf U. Janzen, "The Problem of Piracy in the Newfoundland Fishery in the Aftermath of the War of the Spanish Succession," in *War and Trade in Eighteenth-Century Newfoundland Research in Maritime History*, No. 52 (St. John's, NL: International Maritime Economic History Association, 2013), 31–48.

Anstey, Roger. *The Atlantic Slave Trade and British Abolition, 1760–1810*. London: Macmillan, 1975.

Atkins, J. "A Full and Exact Account of the Tryal of the Pyrates Lately Taken by Captain Ogle, on Board the Swallow Man of War, on the Coast of Guinea." In *British Piracy in the Golden Age: History and Interpretation, 1660–1730*, edited by Joel H. Baer. London: Pickering and Chatto, 2007.

Botting, Douglas. *The Pirates*. New York: Time-Life Books, 1978.

Breverton, Terry. *Black Bart Roberts: The Greatest Pirate of Them All*. Gretna, LA: Pelican Books, 2004.

Bromley, J.S. "The Jacobite Privateers in the Nine Years War." In *Corsairs and Navies: 1660–1760*, 139–65. London: Hambledon, 1987.

Burl, Aubrey. *Black Barty: The Real Pirate of the Caribbean*. Gloucestershire: Sutton, 2006.

Charles River Editors. *The Life and Legacy of Bartholomew Roberts (Black Bart)*. Legendary Pirates. Boston: Harvard Alumnae, 2015.

Conlin, Dan. *Pirates of the Atlantic: Robbery, Murder and Mayhem Off the Canadian East Coast*. Halifax: Formac, 2009.

Cordingly, David. *Life Among the Pirates: The Romance and the Reality*. London: Little, Brown, 1995.

———. *Seafaring Women: Adventures of Pirate Queens, Female Stowaways, and Sailors' Wives*. New York: Random House, 2001.

———. *Under the Black Flag: The Romance and the Reality of Life Among the Pirates*. New York: Harcourt, Brace, 1996.

Earle, Peter. *The Pirate Wars*. New York: St. Martin's Griffin, 2003.

Exquemelin, Alexandre. *The Buccaneers of America*. Translated by Alexis Brown. Harmondsworth, UK: Penguin, 1969.

Gilkerson, William. *Boarders Away: With Steel-Edged Weapons and Polearms*. Lincoln, RI: Andrew Mobray, 1991.

———. *A Thousand Years of Pirates*. Toronto: Tundra Books, 2009.

Gulseth, Chad M. "Back Bart's Ranger." In *Pieces of Eight: More Archaeology of Piracy*, edited by Charles R. Ewen and Russell K. Skowronek. Tallahassee: University Press of Florida, 2016.

Horwood, Harold, and Ed Butts. *Pirates and Outlaws of Canada: 1610 to 1932*. Toronto: Doubleday, 1984.

Johnson, Charles. *A General History of the Pyrates, from Their First Rise and Settlement in the Island of Providence, the Present Time*. 2nd ed. London: T. Warner, 1724.

Klein, Herbert S. *The Atlantic Slave Trade*. 2nd ed. New York: Cambridge University Press, 2010.

Konstam, Angus. *The History of Pirates*. New York: Lyons Press, 1999.

———. *The Pirate Ship 1660–1730*. Oxford: Osprey, 2003.

Lane, Kris E. *Pillaging the Empire: Piracy in the Americas, 1500–1750*. New York: M.E. Sharpe, 1998.

Lincoln, Margarette. *British Pirates and Society, 1680–1730.* London: Ashgate, 2014.

Merriman, R.D. *Queen Anne's Navy: Documents Concerning the Administration if the Navy of Queen Anne, 1702–1714.* London: Navy Records Society, 1961.

Mordal, Jacques. *Twenty-Five Centuries of Sea Warfare.* London: Abbey Library, 1959.

Owen, John Hely. *War at Sea Under Queen Anne, 1702–1708.* New York: Cambridge University Press, 1938.

Pringle, Patrick. *Jolly Roger: The Story of the Great Age of Piracy.* New York: W.W. Norton, 1953.

Pyle, Howard. *The Book of Pirates.* Mineola, NY: Dover, 2000.

———. *Tales of Pirates and Buccaneers.* New York: Random House, 1994.

Rediker, Marcus. *Between the Devil and the Deep Blue Sea: Merchant Seamen, Pirates, and the Anglo-American Maritime World, 1700–1750.* New York: Cambridge University Press, 1987.

———. *Outlaws of the Atlantic: Sailors, Pirates, and Motley Crews in the Age of Sail.* Boston: Beacon Press, 2014.

———. *The Slave Ship: A Human History.* New York: Penguin, 2007.

———. "'Under the Banner of King Death': The Social World of Anglo-American Pirates, 1716 to 1726," *William and Mary Quarterly* 38, no. 2 (1981): 203–27.

———. *Villains of All Nations: Atlantic Pirates in the Golden Age.* Boston: Beacon Press, 2004.

Richards, Stanley. *Black Bart.* Llandybie, Wales: Christopher Davies, 1966.

Rodger, N.A.M. *The Wooden World: An Anatomy of the Georgian Navy.* London: Fontana Press, 1988.

Rogers, Woodes. *Life Aboard a British Privateer in the Time of Queen Anne: Being the Journal of Captain Woodes Rogers, Master Mariner.* Edited by Robert C. Leslie. London: Chapman and Hall, 1889.

Sanders, Richard. *If a Pirate I Must Be …: The True Story of Bartholomew Roberts, King of the Caribbean.* London: Aurum Press, 2007.

Segal, Ronald. *The Black Diaspora: Five Centuries of the Black Experience Outside Africa.* New York: Farrar, Straus and Giroux, 1995.

Shomette, Donald G. *Pirates on the Chesapeake: Being a True History of Pirates, Picaroons, and Raiders on Chesapeake Bay, 1610–1807.* Centreville, MD: Tidewater, 1985.

Snelgrave, William. *A New Account of Some Parts of Guinea and the Slave Trade.* 1734. Reprint, London: Frank Cass, 1971.

Steele, Ian K. *The English Atlantic, 1675–1740: An Exploration of Communication and Community.* New York: Oxford University Press, 1986.

Thomas, Hugh. *The Slave Trade: The Story of the Atlantic Slave Trade: 1440–1870.* New York: Touchstone, 1997.

Tinniswood, Adrian. *Pirates of Barbary: Corsairs, Conquests, and Captivity in the 17th-Century Mediterranean.* New York: Riverhead Books, 2010.

Woodard, Colin. *The Republic of Pirates: Being the True and Surprising Story of the Caribbean Pirates and the Man Who Brought Them Down.* New York: Harcourt, 2007.

Image Credits

Page 89   *The Bay of All Saints* (1664–65) by Joan Blaeu (1596–1673).
Held in the Map Collections, National Library of Brazil.

Page 99   *The West Indies* by Anthony Finley (1790–1840). In Finley,
A., *A New General Atlas; Comprising a Complete Set of Maps,
Representing the Grand Divisions of the Globe, Together with
the Several Empires, Kingdoms and States in the World.*
(Philadelphia: Young and Delleker, 1827).

Page 105   William Henry Rosser, ed., *Coast in the Vicinity of Trepassey
Bay.* Based on surveys in 1764–67 by James Cook and
Michael Lane. In *North Atlantic Directory* (London: n.p.,
1869), page 694. British Library, HMNTS 10496.d.6(1).

Page 128   H. Moll, *A New and Exact Map of Guinea, Divided into ye
Gold, Slave and Ivory Coast, &c. with their Several Kingdoms
and ye Adjacent Countries.* Seventeenth century, reproduced
for Botting, D., ed., *The Pirates* (New York: Time-Life Books,
1978), page 161.

IMAGE CREDITS

Page 132 *Captain Bartho. Roberts with Two Ships, Viz. the* Royal Fortune *and* Ranger, *Taken in Sail in* Whydah *Road on the Coast of* Guinea, *January 11th, 1721/2*, circa 1724. Benjamin Cole, engraver (1695–1764). In Charles Johnson, *A General History of the Pyrates* ... (London: T. Warner, 1724), plate facing page 259.

Page 140 *Portrait of Chaloner Ogle*, circa 1745–47. Unknown artist, British School: Oil on canvas. National Maritime Museum, BHC2917.

Index

Page numbers in italics refer to images.

INDEX

BOOK CREDITS

Acquiring Editor: Carrie Gleason
Developmental Editor: Allison Hirst
Project Editor: Jenny McWha
Copy Editor: Laurie Miller
Proofreader: Ashley Hisson

Cover Designer: Laura Boyle
Interior Designer: Jennifer Gallinger
E-Book Designer: Carmen Giraudy

Publicists: Kendra Martin and Michelle Melski

DUNDURN

Publisher: Kirk Howard
Vice-President: Carl A. Brand
Editorial Director: Kathryn Lane
Vice-President, Design and Production: Jennifer Gallinger
Sales Manager: Synora Van Drine
Publicity Manager: Michelle Melski

Editorial: Allison Hirst, Dominic Farrell, Jenny McWha, Rachel Spence, Elena Radic
Design and Production: Laura Boyle, Carmen Giraudy
Marketing and Publicity: Kendra Martin, Kathryn Bassett

dundurn.com   dundurnpress
@dundurnpress   dundurnpress
dundurnpress   info@dundurn.com

FIND US ON NETGALLEY & GOODREADS TOO!

DUNDURN